Search: Theory and Practice in
Journalism Online

Journalism: Reflections on Practice

Series Editors: **Julian Petley**, Professor of Screen Media, Brunel University, UK
Sarah Niblock, Professor and Head of Journalism, Brunel University, UK

This series provides journalists, academics and students with a unique practical and critical guide to key areas of contemporary journalism practice for the digital age. Each volume offers a local and global perspective, with digital aspects considered throughout. The first series to really synthesise theory with practice, these books will both demonstrate how real-world journalists navigate and accommodate everyday demands, challenges and opportunities in the industry and teach us how to reflect on this.

Published titles:

James Rodgers
REPORTING CONFLICT

Murray Dick
SEARCH: THEORY AND PRACTICE IN JOURNALISM ONLINE

Ros Coward
SPEAKING PERSONALLY

For more information on titles in the series, please visit www.palgrave.com/media/jrp

Series Standing Order
Series ISBN: 978–0–230–58080–0

If you would like to receive future titles in this series as they are published, you can make use of our standing order facility. To place a standing order please contact your bookseller or, in case of difficulty, write to us at the address below with your name and address and the name of the series. Please state with which title you wish to begin your standing order.

Customer Services Department, Macmillan Distribution LTD, Houndmills, Basingstoke, Hampshire, RG21 6XS, UK

Search: Theory and Practice in Journalism Online

Murray Dick

Brunel University, UK

palgrave
macmillan

First published 2013 by
PALGRAVE MACMILLAN

Palgrave Macmillan in the UK is an imprint of Macmillan Publishers Limited,
registered in England, company number 785998, of Houndmills, Basingstoke,
Hampshire RG21 6XS.

Palgrave Macmillan in the US is a division of St Martin's Press LLC,
175 Fifth Avenue, New York, NY 10010.

Palgrave Macmillan is the global academic imprint of the above companies
and has companies and representatives throughout the world.

Palgrave® and Macmillan® are registered trademarks in the United States,
the United Kingdom, Europe and other countries

ISBN: 978-0-230-30189-4

This book is printed on paper suitable for recycling and made from fully
managed and sustained forest sources. Logging, pulping and manufacturing
processes are expected to conform to the environmental regulations of the
country of origin.

A catalogue record for this book is available from the British Library.

A catalog record for this book is available from the Library of Congress.

For my darling Jess, Keir and Tam...

Contents

Preface

The idea for this book first came to me in 2007 while I was at the BBC, working in perhaps the least fashionable (and certainly the least known) of divisions, Information and Archives. While there I developed a specialism in the use of online sources to solve common journalistic problems – finding reliable backgrounders, finding contact details for contributors, verifying contributions from whistleblowers and members of the public. Thousands of contact-hours with hundreds of talented and engaged journalists, not to mention the collective wisdom of the archivists and media researchers who surrounded me, informed my time there. Every page of this book is embellished with this knowledge, and I would like to thank every journalist (and archivist) whom I encountered during that time (and since) for their collective contribution to this work.

As I have moved on from trainer to lecturer and now academic researcher, I have started thinking more about how and why these skills are practiced, and I have sought to make sense of what their use means for modern journalism. This will, I hope, be a legacy of this modest work. Today I find myself the author of a critical account of journalistic practice, a rather fashionable approach in contemporary academe, but one that nonetheless holds much merit for a topic like this. For technologies are prone to obsolescence, and ideas live on. In the drafting of this book, many online sources and software have come and gone (on a tide that will surely continue to ebb and flow in the months and years to come). As time passes, this book will move incrementally away from the cutting edge as online sources disappear, merge or are superseded to become a permanent snapshot of the technologies used by journalists in the second decade of the twenty-first century. As this happens, I hope that the theoretical elements presented here will remain as useful as when they were first committed to a word processing document.

Acknowledgements

The author and publishers would like to thank the following for permission to reproduce copyright material:

Google for screenshots on pages 20, 29, 30

NewsMap for the screenshot on page 35

Blekko for the screenshot on page 37

Information Today for the table on page 41 from Sherman, Chris and Price, Gary (2001) *The Invisible Web: Sources Search Engines Can't See.* Information Today (New Jersey)

Nexis UK for the screenshot on page 50

Cree.py for the screenshot on page 83

Every effort has been made to contact all copyright-holders, but if any have been inadvertently omitted the publishers will be pleased to make the necessary arrangements at the earliest opportunity.

Introduction

The context to this book

It is not often that the process of newsgathering becomes front-page news, yet this was the story that defined late 2011, when David Cameron was compelled to set up the Leveson Inquiry. It is a well-worn cliché that woe betide any journalist who becomes part of the story. But when the way journalists do their job becomes a front-page splash, it seems all too inevitable that serious consequences must follow.

Since 2006, and the publication of the Information Commissioner's report *What Price Privacy?* we have known that British newspapers used illicit means and ways to eke out stories. Journalists, and private investigators working on their behalf, have indulged in unethical means of securing evidence such as payment of witnesses, and illegal methods of obtaining private information, such as phone-hacking and blagging. And yet in a way, it is not these indiscretions and crimes individually which warrant pause for reflection. It is rather a matter of scale.

So frequently were these methods used, they must have seemed like second nature in the newsroom, little different to keeping an eye on the wires, and certainly not a last resort for use in investigations which materially affect society. But just as more on this industrialisation of unethical and criminal practice comes into the public domain, journalists must continue to bring us the news. How do we ensure that newsgathering remains ethically and legally sound, without putting a brake on the way news is made altogether? There seems no better time than now to re-establish the importance of ethical news-gathering as an essential tool in journalism. This book will, I hope, make a useful contribution in this direction.

Many thorny questions arise from news-gathering online, among the wealth of social networks, and other spaces people frequent. To what extent is it fair to use information and files gleaned from social network profiles? Where do we draw a line between private and public information here? What if the user does not fully understand the privacy settings on their social network account?

To further confuse these already thorny issues, we must not forget that social norms are prone to change over time. When W. T. Stead popularised the 'universal interview' as a news-gathering method at the turn of the 20th century, it caused great consternation among the patrician elite of late-Victorian Britain. Henry James, whose distaste for what he termed 'newspaperism', gave voice to this fear: in consenting to this new journalistic device, the masses may do more violence to the dignity of social order than any muckraker ever could (Rubery, 2009). How quaint and stuffy such views seem now, and yet this experience prompts us to consider what future privacy has in the information age, given that the dividing line between private and public space is measured in bits.

The debate about the extent to which online technologies are shaping our notions of privacy rages on. But there is no doubt that the massive (and growing) quantity of information about us online, when aligned with instant access, are changing many facets of modern life. This can be seen in legal areas including libel and contempt of court, in the regulation of use of evidence obtained online, and even in basic professional (and personal) online etiquette.

Can anyone say for certain that the public even care what methods journalists use to bring them their daily read? Given how far-reaching the criminal and extrajudicial investigations around phone-hacking have been, it is perhaps surprising that no large-scale survey has (at the time of writing) been conducted asking the UK public for their thoughts on this and other related issues. But whether or not the public has a say, there remains the not inconsiderable matter of professional propriety to consider.

Anyone who has been engaged in newsgathering professionally knows that it can be a difficult and conflicting business. But it can also be massively rewarding. Those of us who have only ever undertaken legal methods in our newsgathering, and those of us who may have used illicit practices but only as a very last resort when investigating matters of grave public concern, have an obligation to place on public record just how important it is not to abuse the public trust.

But neither must we lose sight of the fact that we live in a democratic and open society. While there are undoubtedly moral issues to be addressed concerning the gathering of information (even information firmly in the public domain), a balance must be struck between privacy and free expression, in the public interest. Open societies require that we know our neighbour, or at least have a means of finding out who they are. The free flow of information is the key to an open and transparent society, and in many ways the internet is a particularly apt medium to help us realise transparency in our public and social affairs.

What this book is not

This book does not start from the premise that everyone has something to hide, or that 'privacy is for peados' (Williams, 2011).

This book is not a muckraker's manual – it does not assume that there is something intrinsically 'fishy' about those who happen to be in the news. On the contrary, ethical questions permeate every aspect of a journalist's working life, and so by extension, ethical criteria must govern the acquisition and use of online resources. From the gathering, to the management, to the distribution of information found online, there is more to questioning how journalists should do their work, than merely how quickly.

It has been argued that declining trust in newspapers is a major factor in declining circulations, a position which has been strengthened by the sort of truths the Leveson Inquiry has laid bare. Others feel that the audience is, whether willingly or unwillingly, complicit in the conspiracy, and that trust has no bearing on why punters part with their cash. Others still argue that the media habits of the public are governed more by the possibilities of choice wrought by new technologies and mediums, than by loyalty to a particular source of news. Wherever the truth lies, and whatever the state of the industry, it behoves any journalist to act with dignity and decorum, whether because this is how we would wish to be treated ourselves, or because such behaviour brings its own virtue.

That said, this book is not a philosophical treatise. While an analysis of the Categorical Imperative may tell us much about life and the universe, it tells us little specific about the practice of journalism, which is central to this book. Ethical issues are therefore framed very much around analysing the practices, guidelines and lessons learned in the field, and in other related or similar professional fields.

Theory is explored in this book as a means of anchoring online resources and tools to the context in which they were developed. The technologies which define this field are prone to change, and obsolescence, often in a very short period of time. But while many of the resources covered in the following pages will be mothballed in the months and years ahead, the thinking and use which make them such invaluable resources in the first place, will remain.

Use of this book

This book offers a practical overview of the journalistic potential in various new (and developing) online tools, informed by several related theoretical fields.

The internet is a fast-changing environment, in which journalists must play catch-up in response to emerging online resources. But modern journalism is also a high-pressure environment. Converging industries and media, and increasing competition from non-traditional media in breaking news, make it more and more important that journalists are skilled in effective and efficient search methods.

But the emergence of these technologies also requires a re-appraisal of key theoretical issues, that inform and are informed by practice.

Whether uncovering breaking stories, finding reliable background on ongoing stories, or finding witnesses and contributors, today there is a wealth of information freely available at journalists' fingertips. But these tools arrive in a messy and unstructured way, and it is not always easy to know where to find them, let alone learn how to use them.

The new social web offers journalists a means of collaboration with fellow professionals, experts and sources (not to mention the 'former audience'), which can revolutionise the research process, but this in turn requires an informed debate around several theoretical issues.

References

Rubery, Matthew (2009) *The Novelty of Newspapers*. Oxford University Press: Oxford.

Williams, Olivia (2011) 'Privacy Is For Paedos' Paul McMullan Shocks Leveson Inquiry Over Hacking Culture, Huffington Post, November 30: http://www. huffingtonpost.co.uk/2011/11/29/notw-journalist-paul-mcmu_n_1118764. html

1 Search in theory

Information overload is a modern concept, though not a new one. Long pre-dating the rise of the internet, the term was popularised by Alvin Toffler. His book, *Future Shock* (1984), conveyed the *nausea* of the information age, and the sense of dislocation individuals and groups feel as a result of excessive change in a too short period of time. The concept has been studied and analysed in a range of information professions, from accounting to marketing and consumer research. In most cases the common denominator is that individual performance (in terms of decision-making) varies relative to the volume of information available, up to a point. Beyond that relative point, further information results in rapidly declining performance (Eppler and Mengis, 2004).

As far back as 1997, information overload was found to interfere with journalists' ability to gain traction, or 'grip' over the news (Nicholas and Martin, 1997). Journalists have complained of information overload caused by modern working life, and not least excessive PR communications, or 'information subsidy' (Curtin, 1999). More recently, scholars have predicted that information overload will continue to be a key challenge for journalist and citizen alike in today's networked world (Servaes, 2009).

The internet makes it possible for anyone to publish information, which has led to rapid growth in the production of information online. Indeed, Google indexed its landmark trillionth web page as far back as 2008. This sea of information can be disorientating without adequate support, and the risk of misinformation to journalists poses a serious danger to professional credibility.

Information overload continues to inspire new literature, albeit at a declining rate since around 2004. Some critics have argued that the volume of information on the internet is making us more 'stupid' (Carr, 2010), others disagree (Battelle, 2008). Striking a pragmatic note, Shirky (2008) turned the concept of information overload on its head, arguing that the true malaise of the modern era is rather 'filter failure'. This is conceived as the collapse of those systems we use to help us tell good from bad (the likes of which we make use of everyday in our off-line lives). While on the surface this may seem a mere semantic twist, Shirky's term moves us away from the individual (not 'user') as a help-less, information 'junkie'. It moves us instead towards a place where, if we can build filters online to help determine the useful from the useless more efficiently, then we may be able to plot a course through this sea of information.

This book will offer an overview of the current state of information filters available to journalists working online. It is intended to help jour-nalists address the filter failure that plagues contemporary, networked journalism.

How journalists use the internet

Throughout the last century, most large media organisations employed teams of researchers and librarians whose job was to provide journalists with research systems (such as newspaper clippings) and a full reference library service. A combination of economic factors (including declining circulations and industry consolidation) and technological developments (including the emergence of powerful and affordable database technolo-gies) have changed this. As with many other professions throughout the global economy, media research is increasingly becoming the domain of the all singing, all dancing all-rounder: the journalist.

Today many journalists do much of their own research from the comfort of a desk. But navigating the internet as a researcher or journal-ist is a different proposition from using it to book holidays and listen to music. One difference is that a journalist cannot just give up on a story if he/she is struggling to find the information needed, another is that the news schedule will not slow down to accommodate journalists who cannot find information in time.

Various studies have considered how journalists use the internet to help them source news and contributors. Nicholas (1996) found that Guardian journalists (who demonstrated degrees of capability in online search) were not as ignorant of technique as some librarians (and librar-ianship literature) assumed them to be.

The mid-1990s saw a tipping point in US journalists' usage of the web in newsgathering. One study found that daily use of the internet had risen from 25% of respondents in 1994 to 92.4% in 1998 (Garrison,

1999). This rise in usage has fuelled concerns about the content found online, especially concerning the verifiability and reliability of this information.

By 2001 web search was out-stripping the use of commercial online research tools in US journalists' news-gathering routines (Garrison, 2001), and by 2005, it was found that almost two-thirds of journalists were using competitor news found on the web in their research and reporting (EURO RSCG Magnet & Columbia University, 2005). However, just because journalists today have access to many unofficial sources online does not mean they use them. On the contrary, the old long-established 'conventional' means of sourcing stories remains (Jha, 2007).

More recent studies have moved away from the basic measurement of internet use, towards trying to understand the contexts within which the internet is accessed by journalists. This includes issues arising out of professional context, such as time constraints, and means of access, in terms of the range of tools available to journalists, and those which are actually used (Hermans et al., 2009). While it is important not to confuse professional approach with medium in journalism, online journalists have been found to be more trusting of news they find online than print journalists (Cassidy, 2007), suggesting a relationship between the two.

In perhaps the most comprehensive research study to date into journalists' use of online search tools, Machill and Beiler (2009) found that although Google plays a decisive role in most German journalists' news-gathering research today, it is nevertheless one of relatively few online tools commonly used in the newsroom. They found that most journalists achieve only moderate levels of success in online search. Those who apply most thought to search problems were found to perform best overall. It was also found that journalists' concerns about the reliability and verifiability of material found on the web have led to an increase in the cannibalistic approach to newsgathering that journalists will tend to reference their own work and other media at the expense of reflecting the whole web. Further research has shown that just over half of journalists are oblivious to blogs and social media in terms of sourcing the news (Oriella PR Network, 2011).

Search theory

Morville (2005) explains that the central issue in search (or 'information retrieval' as it was originally known) has traditionally been the concept of *relevance*. Traditionally, developers in this field have conceptualised search in terms of the binary (and inversely related) concepts of 'precision' and 'recall' as measures of *relevance*. These two concepts have very precise meanings in search engine development, thus:

Precision = Number of relevant and retrieved/Total number retrieved
Recall = Number of relevant and retrieved/Total number relevant
(Morville, 2005, p. 51)

Morville goes on to explain these concepts in the following terms: 'precision measures how well a system retrieves only the relevant documents... recall measures how well a system retrieves all the relevant documents' (Morville, 2005, p. 49). How important these two concepts are (and how search strategy should be amended to accommodate them) depends on the type of search undertaken. For searches which require a certain (manageable) number of search results (a situation common to many busy, time-poor news journalists), precision is the key. But for exhaustive searches, where unearthing a fact may require hours of painstaking search (a situation most investigative journalists will be able to relate to) recall is the key.

But this approach is fundamentally compromised by the imprecision, ambiguity and vagueness of language as it is used by one variable which no laboratory conditions can impose order upon, the searcher. When *relevance* is defined by search engines, it is an aggregate, quantitative measure, whereas we humans think of relevance in a rather more fluid, ambiguous, qualitative way. This is why search requires additional *aboutness*, and additional keywords for content, not to mention Boolean operators, field-specific functions and other advanced options.

In the mid-1990s, the focus of work in information retrieval moved away from the hard science of precision and recall, and towards the study of how humans interact with information (Bates, 2002). Putting the searcher at the centre of the process changes the landscape. Acknowledging that information needs to evolve as searchers interact with the tools at their disposal (and change their search needs) changes the game.

Search developers are aware of the importance of iteration in search that what is considered to be the right result is an (often) internalised process of negotiation. Expert search is akin to *berrypicking* in that it is discriminating (Bates, 2002). Users *satisfice* their search needs. As such, those search options which are available to us can change the nature not only of what can be found, but also of what we seek (Halavais,

2009, p. 87). Post-modernity, it could be argued, came late to search, but information literacy can help journalists to clear a path through the search wilderness.

How search engines work

The term 'search engine' is often used to refer to two entirely different types of search resource, human-powered directories (which will be covered in more detail later in this book) and crawler-based search engines. The first form, human-powered directories, such as the Open Directory Project, DMOZ (http://www.dmoz.org/), are designed to aid browsing for information within a collection of materials organised along the lines of human expertise, and presented in an intuitive way.

The second form, crawler-based search engines like Google, Bing and Yahoo, have three components. First is the 'spider', the algorithms which pass through the internet looking for new content and for changes to existing content. This process involves analysing all information on a page, parsing that information, and then storing it in the second component, the search engine's 'index'. The 'spider' then exits via the links found on that page, so if a web page has been spidered but not indexed, it will not be found via the search engine. The third component, the search engine, is a program which helps the searcher interact with the index, and which ranks content returned in terms of 'relevance'.

Major search engines differ only by degrees, in particular with regard to the metrics (and the weighting of these metrics) used to determine 'relevance'.

Google is said to use over 200 'signals' to help determine the relevance ranking of web pages, including their patented PageRank algorithm (which uses co-citation between web pages to inform ranking). However, apart from some general technical (and editorial) advice, the company is deliberately vague on how these signals are weighted in ranking. This absence of transparency is deliberate; it stems from not wishing to give unscrupulous web publishers ammunition with which to 'game' the system (Moran and Hunt, 2006). This is a fast changing situation. Some of those methods which have been significant in search relevance in the past, such as the use of metadata tags to add meaning to online content, have been exploited by 'spammers' and so their significance in ranking has been muted. For example, the <Keywords> HTML meta tag is no longer factored into ranking (Cutts, 2009).

More recently, Google has been forced to acknowledge the need to move towards qualitative notions of quality and relevance. The 'Panda' algorithm (Google Blog, 2011), has been developed in the midst of wide-ranging concern about the rise of 'content farms', websites whose content is optimised for search, but which owe their online authority more to effective exploitation of Google's Adsense marketing platform, than to reputation for providing quality information (Roth, 2009).

Political economy of search

Jurgen Habermas conceived of the public sphere as a social arena which exists between the private sphere of enterprise and the government. It is somewhere people can get together to talk openly about the issues of the day, to debate social problems, and organise action accordingly. This neo-Enlightenment concept, it is argued, found its apogee in the coffee houses of 17th and 18th century London. These were discursive spaces, places where deliberative democracy could flourish (Habermas, 1991). But does the economic structure and technology comprising today's search industry contribute to, or detract from this ideal?

Monopolies and oligopolies, in effect at least, abound within the search industry. In July 2010, Google domains accounted for more than 90% of the UK search market (Experian Hitwise Data Center, 2010) – an effective monopoly unrivalled in virtually any other industry. But Google has a major influence upon the information we consume due to search behaviour too. Research on AOL server logs has found that 42% of users click on the first placed result in search engine results, while only 12% click on the second placed result and 9% on the third. The first ten results receive 90% of all click-through traffic, and the second page only just over 4% (Enge et al., 2010). People do not have the time or resources to check every result, and as the internet grows we are becoming more dependent upon Google as an arbiter of relevance (as a proxy for *truth*) in our lives.

Google's corporate literature used to describe the PageRank algorithm as 'uniquely democratic'; a claim which has led some in academe to question just what kind of democratic system the company have developed. In a theoretical consideration of search indexing method, Introna and Nissenbaum (2000) argued that far from being an egalitarian domain, a small number of elite online sources dominate on the web. Elsewhere, those concerned with deliberative democracy have argued that Google's PageRank algorithm has a less democratic sense of relevance than the company may like us to believe. Commercial motivation drives content creation on search engines according to Hargittai (2004), who argues that there is an association between the economic might of corporate firms and the influencing of search rankings (albeit no empirical data was provided to corroborate this view). On the other hand, it has been argued that the imperfection of current state search engines means that searchers can actually benefit from serendipity (Lev-On, 2008).

Challenging those who claim that the internet (as represented by the PageRank method of link citation) is 'inherently democratic', Diaz draws upon empirical research by Barabási (2002), which found that the Web's structure is far from egalitarian in nature, but is rather organised around a small number of elite 'hubs' – a process described as the 'rich get richer' phenomenon (Diaz, 2008). Well-linked web pages benefit from more and more links (as they are easy to find), and so entrenchment bias or 'Googlearchy' prevails. What started with the professionalisation of information has now led to information industrialisation and it is argued, to a crude utilitarianism expressed in the 'digital version of the vox populi' (Hinman, 2008, p. 67).

One rather obvious manifestation of bias online is censorship, and Google's attempts to censor material in countries around the world, in order to accord with law (and in some cases government whim). While it could be argued that the censorship of anti-semitic material in France and Germany is justified, it is harder to excuse the fact that references to Taiwan independence and Tianenmen Square have been censored in the Chinese version of Google. Indeed, it has been argued further that the local versions of 'search' Google has established around the world making it easier to enforce censorship locally (Halavais, 2009). So relevance, as established by factoring in country-specific factors into search ranking, can work counter to the truth.

Diaz conceives of search engines as 'general interest intermediaries' (Diaz, 2008, p. 15), which should be scrutinised in the same way as any other mass media organisation. But Hinman goes further still, arguing that search engines 'construct knowledge through control of access' (Hinman, 2008, p. 73). Our public trust rests in the hands of a commercial body whose imperative to thwart industrial espionage by keeping the ranking recipe secret, mean we can never judge for ourselves whether or not bias exists: '...the political possibilities of the Web are constrained by its architecture. The end-to-end design of the Web might not limit the political sites that citizens visit, but the link structure of the Web certainly does' (Hindman, 2009, p. 57). Others, of course, would counter that it is unfair (and indeed patronising) to play down the agency of searchers (or web authors) in the process of search.

Search and privacy

Among the 200 signals Google uses to rank search results, are elements defined as 'contextual relevance'. These relate to personal information about a searcher and their search habits, and may include location, search history, profile data and language preferences. It may even include the *bounce rate* for links clicked on (a measure of user time spent on a page before returning to search results – the less time spent dwelling on a page, the less 'relevant' the link clicked on is considered to be). There is disagreement within industry upon the degree to which these factors impact on relevance, but personal information is undoubtedly a factor in relevance.

In imagining the 'perfect search engine', Zimmer (2008) put forth a theoretical axis of relevance driven by two mutually inclusive concepts: 'perfect reach' and 'perfect recall'. The former necessitates access to all available information and the latter comprises personally relevant, bespoke search results. But achieving 'perfect recall' would require search engines to harvest more and more of our personal information (such as contextual relevance), which in turn represents a threat to our personal privacy. Eric Goldman (2006) re-framed this issue, claiming that the subjective, changing and secretive approach to search engine relevance, which he termed 'search bias', is both necessary and desirable as a public good, insofar as it reduces information overload. It is inevitable, he further argues, that this bias will be consigned to the dustbin of history by the rise of personalised search results.

More recent critiques argue that the rise of personalisation (whether that be via contextual factors, search history or friend's recommendations in search) can dampen the effects of search bias. This means of determining 'relevance', it is argued, has the potential to cause the wider public to become intellectually complacent and quiescent. In this view, personalisation represents a pernicious cultural relativism that cocoons us all from competing or opposing truths, trapping us in our own beliefs and prejudices. This, it is argued, impoverishes us all insofar as we are instantly removed from opinions and facts which may challenge our most basic assumptions (Pariser, 2011).

In turn Pariser's assumptions have been questioned. Morozov (2011, I) critiques Pariser's utopian belief that internet companies should do anything other than provide a means of finding things out. On the contrary, he argues 'algorithms do not "think" – they compute. And while computing the "is" (i.e. relevance) is something they can accomplish, computing the "ought" (i.e. our information duties as citizens) is a much more contentious and value-laden process'. (Morozov, 2011, I). But on the other hand, it may equally be countered that the weighting of the 200 'signals' Google uses to determine relevance owe more to editorial judgement (as found in any newsroom), than to the lightening-quick processing of zeros and ones. Morozov takes after Goldman in arguing that regulatory intervention may create more problems than it solves, for what makes one bias better than any other? (Morozov, 2011, II). And yet left to their own devices search engine companies only have to do the bare minimum in order to protect our privacy.

In 2009 Tim Berners Lee voiced concern about 'behavioural targeting' in search, arguing that our quality of life may be adversely affected where our search history is factored into our ability to buy life assurance, or work (Poulter, 2009). For journalists freedom of expression is a direct concern too. In the US, The Patriot Act (2001) has led to state intrusion into search habits. Internet search histories have been used in the prosecution of alleged terrorists (Graham, 2009) while in the UK, the Prevention of Terrorism Act (2006) includes a positive obligation to report information which may materially assist the authorities in preventing terrorism (something any journalist may stumble across when researching sensitive issues). In other circumstance, the loss of privacy in search can lead to the identification of dissidents and proscribed groups. In the wrong hands this can pose a challenge to freedom of expression, and even a risk to life. For this reason, it is important that journalists know how to protect their search privacy should they need to work on a sensitive topic.

For journalists who are concerned about intrusions into their search (especially with regard to investigative journalism in the public interest), the best option is to use an encrypted (proxy) Internet Connection, ideally via a reputable proxy system such as Tor (https://www.torproject.org/), and to use an anonymising, private search engine in conjunction with this software, like DuckDuckGo (http://duckduckgo.com/).

But it is not just a journalists' own search history that can raise ethical problems. The search term prompts offered by Google Suggest are based on volumes of past search queries, and they represent an interesting quandary for journalists. On the one hand, this function can speed up search, and can even form the basis of original research and journalism. Search trends have been used to anticipate crises as they develop, such as the Mexican swine flu outbreak in 2009 (Madrigal, 2009), and they have been used by the Bank of England to tap into indicators of economic growth (McLaren, 2011). But equally they can lead to a certain circularity of thought – where the dominant terms and language used can unduly influence individual search at an atomic, pervasive level. Knowing how and when to switch this option off is just as important as knowing when to step back from journalistic cliché in the process of writing.

References

Barabási, Albert-László (2002) *Linked: The New Science of Networks*. Perseus Publishing: Cambridge.

Bates, Marcia (2002) 'Toward an Integrated Model of Information Seeking and Searching' (Keynote Address, Fourth international Conference on Information Needs, Seeking and Use in Different Contexts, Lisbon, Portugal, September 11, 2002), *New Review of Information Behaviour Research*, 3, 1–15.

Battelle, John (2008) Google: Making Nick Carr Stupid, But It's Made This Guy Smarter, Searchblog, June 10: http://battellemedia.com/archives/2008/06/google_making_nick_carr_stupid_but_its_made_this_guy_smarter#ixzz1O1maEKdZ

Carr, Nicholas (2008) 'Is Google making us stupid?', *Atlantic Magazine*, July/August: http://www.theatlantic.com/magazine/archive/2008/07/is-google-making-us-stupid/6868/

Cassidy, William P. (2007) 'Online News Credibility: An Examination of the Perceptions of Newspaper Journalists', *Journal of Computer-Mediated Communication*, 12, 478–498.

Curtin, Paul (1999) 'Re-evaluating Public Relations Information Subsidies: Market-Driven Journalism and Agenda-Building Theory and Practice', *Journal of Public Relations Research*, 11(1), 53–90.

Cutts, Matt (2009) 'Google doesn't use the keywords meta tag in web search', Matt Cutts Blog, September 21: http://www.mattcutts.com/blog/keywords-meta-tag-in-web-search/

Diaz, A (2008) 'Through the Google Googles: Sociopolitical Bias in Search Engine Design', in Spink, Amanda and Zimmer, Michael (eds), *Web Search: Multidisciplinary Perspectives*. Springer: Berlin.

Enge, Eric; Spencer, Stephen; Fishkin, Rand and Stricchiola, Jessie (2010) *The Art of SEO: Mastering Search Engine Optimization*, Sebastapol: O'Reilly.

Eppler, Martin J. and Mengis, Jeanne (2004) 'The Concept of Information Overload: A review of Literature from Organization Science, Accounting, Marketing, MIS and Related Disciplines', *The Information Society*, 20, 325–344.

EURO RSCG Magnet & Columbia University Survey of the Media (2005) Rebuilding trust: Can credibility be rebuilt in the newsroom and the boardroom. Retrieved May 31, 2006 from http://magnet.mediaroom.com/file.php/binaries/31/RebuildingTrust.pdf

Experian Hitwise Data Center (2010) 'Top Sites & Engines': http://www.hitwise.com/uk/datacentre/main/dashboard-7323.html

Garrison, Bruce (1999) 'Journalists' Perceptions of Online Information-Gathering Problems' A paper presented to the Newspaper Division of the Association for Education in Journalism and Mass Communication, Southeast Colloquium, Lexington, March 5–6.

Garrison, Bruce (2001) 'Diffusion of Online Information Technologies in Newspaper', *Newsrooms Journalism*, 2(2), 2 221–239.

Goldman, Eric (2006) 'Search Engine Bias and the Demise of Search Engine Utopianism', in Spink, Amanda and Zimmer, Michael (eds), *Web Search: Multidisciplinary Perspectives*. Springer: Berlin.

Google (2011) Company Philosophy – Ten Things: http://www.google.com /about/corporate/company/tenthings.html

Google Blog (2011) Finding more high-quality sites in search, February 24: http://googleblog.blogspot.com/2011/02/finding-more-high-quality-sites-in.html

Graham, Kevin (2009) 'Testimony Centers On 'USEF' Internet Searches', *St Petersberg Times*, Florida, August 20.

Habermas, Jurgen (1991) *The Structural Transformation of the Public Sphere: An Inquiry into a Category of Bourgeois Society*. The MIT Press: New York.

Halavais, Alexander (2009) *Search Engine Society*. Polity Press: London.

Hargittai, Eszter, (2004). 'Do you "google"? Understanding Search Engine Popularity Beyond the Hype', *First Monday*, 9(3).

Hermans, Liesbeth; Vergeer, Maurice; and Pleijter, Alexander (2009) 'Internet Adoption in the Newsroom: Journalists' Use of the Internet Explained by Attitudes and Perceived Functions', *Communications*, 34(1), 55–71.

Hindman, Matthew (2009) *The Myth of Digital Democracy*. Princeton University Press: Oxford.

Hinman, Lawrence (2008) 'Searching Ethics: The Role of Search Engines in the Construction and Distribution of Knowledge', in Spink, Amanda and Zimmer, Michael (eds) *Web Search: Multidisciplinary Perspectives*. Springer: Berlin.

Introna, Lucas and Nissenbaum, Helen (2000) Shaping the Web: Why the politics of search engines matters: www.nyu.edu/projects/nissenbaum/papers/search-engines.pdfSimilar

Jha, Sonora (2007) Exploring Internet Influence on the Coverage of Social Protest: Content Analysis, *Journalism and Mass Communication Quarterly*, Spring 2007; 84, 1; ABI/INFORM Research pages 40–57.

Lev-On, Azi (2008) 'The Democratizing Effects of Search Engine Use: On Chance Exposure and Organizational Hubs', in Spink, Amanda and Zimmer, Michael (eds) *Web Search: Multidisciplinary Perspectives*. Springer: Berlin.

Machill, Marcel and Beiler, Markus (2009) 'The Importance of the Internet for Journalistic Research', *Journalism Studies*, 10(2), 178–203.

Madrigal, Alex (2009) Google Could Have Caught Swine Flu Early, Wired.com, April 29: http://www.wired.com/wiredscience/2009/04/google-could-have-caught-swine-flu-early/

McLaren, Nick (2011) Using Internet Search Data as economic indicators, *Bank of England Quarterly Bulletin*, Q2: http://www.bankofengland.co.uk/publications /quarterlybulletin/qb110206.pdf

Moran, Mike and Hunt, Bill (2006) *Search Engine Marketing (2nd Edition)*. London: IBM Press.

Morozov, Evgeny (2011, I) Your Own Facts (book review of The Filter Bubble, by Eli Pariser), New York Times, June 10: http://www.nytimes.com/2011/06/12/books/review/book-review-the-filter-bubble-by-eli-pariser.html?_r=1

Morozov, Evgeny (2011, II) *The Net Delusion: How not to Liberate the World*. Allen Lane: London.

Morville, Peter (2005) *Ambient Findability*. O'Reilly: Sebastopol.

Nicholas, Dave (1996) 'An assessment of the Online Searching Behaviour of Practioner end Users', *Journal of Documentation*, 52(3), 227–251.

Nicholas, Dave and Martin, Helen (1997) 'Assessing Information Needs: A Case Study of Journalists', *Aslib Proceedings*, 49(2), 43–52.

Oriella PR Network (2011) Click, Community and Conversations: The State of Journalism in 2011, Digital Journalism Study: http://www.orielladigitaljournalism.com/view-report.html#/4/

Pariser, Eli (2011) *The Filter Bubble: What The Internet Is Hiding From You*. Penguin Press: London.

Poulter, Sean (2009) Internet ad tracking system will put a 'spy camera' in the homes of millions, warns founder of the web, *Daily Mail*, March 12: http://www.dailymail.co.uk/news/article-1161215/Internet-ad-tracking-spy-camera-homes-millions-warns-founder-web.html#ixzz1K44kJYur

Roth, Daniel (2009) The Answer Factory: Demand Media and the Fast, Disposable, and Profitable as Hell Media Model, *Wired Magazine*, October 19: http://www.wired.com/magazine/2009/10/ff_demandmedia/

Servaes, Jan (2009) 'We are all journalists now!', *Journalism*,10(3), 371–374.

Shirky, Clay (2008) 'It's Not Information Overload, It's Filter Failure', talk at Web 2.0 Expo New York City, September 2008: http://blip.tv/web2expo/web-2-0-expo-ny-clay-shirky-shirky-com-it-s-not-information-overload-it-s-filter-failure-1283699

Toffler, Alvin (1984) *Future Shock*. Bantam: New York.

Zimmer, Michael (2008) 'The Externalities of Search 2.0: The Emerging Privacy Threats when the Drive for the Perfect Search Engine meets Web 2.0', *First Monday*, 13(3).

2 Search in practice

Approaches to search

In the previous chapter we considered how search engines work, and how 'search engine' is an umbrella term for different types of search resources (specifically between those sources such as human-powered directories, or structured collections of links to materials which encourage browsing, and crawler-based search programs which allow you to keyword search an index). These different types of resources encourage different approaches to search, and the different types of searches we undertake in order to satisfy search needs. If what you are searching for exists within a hierarchy for example, it may be better to browse for the answer using a directory, rather than using a search engine. Of course there are many different types of search engines, some of which index material which is more appropriate for some searches than for others. Where searching general search engines fails to yield positive results, you may want to opt for a specialist search engine or site.

Browsing, or searching?

A very basic search strategy involves weighing up (in a non-scientific way) the concepts of precision and recall introduced in the previous chapter, and establishing which is more important in the search need. It may be said that most day-to-day search queries will have more emphasis on precision than on recall. The time constraints and transient nature of news journalism means that the accuracy of search results relative to search query is more important than their exhaustiveness. However this is not uniformly the case – anyone who has ever worked in negative checks (checking the names of fictitious characters against real people), or anyone who has undertaken investigative online search, will more likely than not require results weighed more towards recall than precision. In turn, knowing which concept drives *relevance* in your search need can inform appropriate use of advanced operators and functions, whether the searcher should opt for those which restrict, or those which expand the flow of results.

Online search expert, Nora Paul suggests that surfers should let their strategy be guided by what most journalists will recognise as Kipling's *Six honest serving men*: Who, What, When, Where, Why, How (Schlein, 2004). This approach can be used to focus on those keywords and phrases to use in search.

Alternatively, visualising the (hypothetical) information you want, in the words you would expect to find them on the page (or document), can be useful. This will help with establishing keywords, though may involve a good deal of imaginative leg-work, depending on the search query. It is helpful to think about this from a document analysis perspective:

Who (or what kind of person) may be the author of the words you are looking for? Is it someone whose educational/social/demographic profile explicitly impacts the words and language that they use (and that you will need to search for)?

Is it published in a source whose formal style can be mined for clues as to which words to search for (Manchester United footballer Wayne Rooney is routinely referred to as *Roo* or *Wazza* in UK tabloid newspapers, but referred to as Rooney in the broadsheet press). This should also help inform the keywords used.

Is it written in the first, second, or third person? Although Google (and other search engines) compensate for grammatical variation in search terms (such as tense), it is possible that some keywords are conceptualised differently according to who is saying them.

Is there more than one answer to any of the above questions? If so, this may also impact choice of search terms.

In terms of choosing search terms, it is always useful to make use of a thesaurus, or even a subject directory (depending on your subject and approach). Trying to avoid words with multiple meanings will help with precision. If that is not possible, try incorporating those terms into a phrase, to avoid passing references to homonyms.

Search engine marketing professionals categorise queries into three distinct categories, which they use to design the information architecture of web pages more effectively. The three categories of search intent are:

Transactional: search queries which suggest the surfer is using the search engine to try to do something. For example, the search term *video* would suggest the searcher wants to buy a video.

Informational: search queries which suggest the surfer is trying to find something out. For example, *where is Osama Bin Laden buried* would suggest the searcher is looking for information.

Navigational: search queries which suggest the surfer is trying to get to a particular website. For example a search for *bbc news* would suggest that the searcher is looking for the BBC news website. (Thurow and Musica, 2009)

It may therefore be instructive for searchers to consider whether their searches are informational or transactional before searching. This may in turn inform the sort of approach to search taken.

Alternatively, there are some things not directly related to online research, but which nevertheless have an impact on search success. Calishain (2005) identifies an approach to search in this vein as 'the principle of every scrap'. A methodical and meticulous approach to online search, it is argued, is just as important for difficult search needs, as it is the process of searching itself. Keeping a solid account of what you have done is the key. This might include:

Saving or bookmarking relevant related material.

Recording the keywords used to find these resources.

Analysing the types of website returned for your searches (by domain, or other criteria).

Without these records, you stand doomed either to miss out on things you have forgotten to search for, or to go round and round in circles doing the same searches again and again.

Henninger (2008) offers some useful general advice on searching online, suggesting that searchers should:

1. Develop a firm concept of what you are looking for – write it down.
2. List synonyms or phrases that reflect each concept.
3. Select the appropriate tool – internet, known web server, database vendor or reference tool.
4. No matter which searching tool, use advanced searching techniques and take advantage of its special features.

5. Examine the titles, summaries and/or contents of documents found to see if they are relevant to your request.
6. If they are not relevant then refine the search by modifying the strategy to get a list of documents that are more relevant.
7. If not enough documents are found, modify the strategy to increase the number of relevant documents retrieved.
8. If you do not find anything relevant, try a different research tool (return to step 6).

(Henninger, 2008, p. 91)

Screen breaks

One last piece of advice which is very important – it is wise to take regular screen breaks between searching sessions. Unless you keep a clear and focussed mind, it is easy to become distracted by irrelevant material, which drag you further from your search goal, and which eats away valuable time. Screen breaks give the opportunity to pause and reflect – which can be essential when undertaking large-scale, or frequent online search tasks.

Advanced searching Google

The simplest way to refine a search in Google (or any search engine) is simply to use more terms, because the more terms you add, the less results you will get back. This is equivalent to the AND operator in Boolean Logic, a means of formal logic, or search grammar, which

Google's advanced search interface

can help to shape the relationship between words in a search query. In Google the AND function is implicit in the space between two keywords. But adding more words to your search can be taxing, and overly restrictive. For this reason it is a good idea to avail yourself of the many other operators and functions available in Google, which can help either refine or expand a search. Here is an overview of the key operators and functions, and how you can use them.

OR (|): When you are searching for something which can be expressed in more than one way, it can be useful to run an 'OR' search using a range of terms. For example, using either the pipe symbol (|) or the upper-case word OR here:

blair wmd OR weapons.

...will return pages containing the word blair and either weapons, or the acronym WMD.

NOT (-): Just as you can add keywords to your search string, so too can you remove them if they are distorting your results. For example, were you to search for *rangers*, with the aim of finding pages on Glasgow Rangers, you might want to remove references to other sporting teams with Rangers in their title, such as Texas Rangers, Queens Park Rangers (QPR) etc. Hence:

rangers -texas -qpr

It is worth noting, however, that using the NOT function too often can, in some cases, inadvertently filter out relevant content from your search. It is perfectly possible, for example, that the information you seek is available on a long, narrative, textual page which references both Glasgow *Rangers* and *QPR*, but paragraphs apart (say, essays on British football).

Phrase search (" "): When searching for terms which are likely to appear contiguously, in a particular order, it is wise to use phrase searching. Searching for *Putin Berlusconi*, for example, is not as precise or as restrictive as:

"putin and berlusconi"

Phrase searching can be a little restrictive however – so in this case, a safer bet to find articles which are expressly about the relationship between Putin and Berlusconi, the search would be better put as:

"putin and berlusconi" OR "berlusconi and putin"

Phrase searching is also important when the expression you are concerned with contains a stop word (common words such as, *is*, *that*, *and* and *to*) which Google (and other search engines) tend to ignore when you search.

Phrase searching also supports a means of applying one aspect of search theory covered in the last chapter. It is possible to use phrase searching to answer hypothetical questions you may have in your search results, by searching for a fragment of language you would expect to find in answer to your question. So for example if you wanted to find reference to the UK's wealthiest banker, try searching for...

"UK's wealthiest banker"

...which may appear in the answer, where it is phrased "the UK's wealthiest banker is...".

Phrase searching also allows you to force keywords. Google tends to ignore any common words used in search because in many circumstances they do not help refine a search query. In addition, because Google's PageRank algorithm is a principal factor in Google ranking, sometimes pages which do not actually contain all your search terms, but most of them, and that have other pages linking to them containing your remaining words, will be included in your results. This is one reason why you may not always find the keywords you searched for on the pages you have returned.

To ensure Google includes such words in your search results, place in double quotes ("") any word you insist should feature in the search results. This approach also blocks Google from automatically stemming your words, that is, finding your keyword with different conjugations or word endings. This is useful if you are interested in a word in a particular case, or tense. Though you may be able to force Google to show you any particular word, Google ignores all but a tiny handful of characters, including "%", "$", "\", ".", "@", "#", and "+" (Google, 2012), and it is case insensitive (Long, 2005).

Synonyms (~): The tilde operator can be used to take advantage of Google's internal thesaurus, if you seek other terms related to those you are searching for. For example, ~*marriage* will return related concepts which include references to *love*, *weddings,* etc. This can be useful in many searches, especially where the terminology you would expect to find used is fluid (and non-specialist language). At the time of writing this function is not supported in all languages (e.g. there is no Russian equivalent), but is available by default in some personalised search results. The synonym operator can be thought of as being diametrically opposite to the + operator in terms of results returned – it improves recall, but in an intuitive way, by exploiting the conceptual similarity between words.

Wildcard (*): Many search engines allow you to employ a wildcard operator which can be used as substitute for a particular letter (or a number of letters) where you are unsure how a certain word may be spelled by the sources you are searching for. Google does not support the wildcard used in this way because it uses an internal thesaurus to provide automatic stemming to find alternate word-endings and spellings for your terms. In Google you can use a * when phrase searching in order to serve as a placeholder for a word which could be one of many alternatives. This can be useful in some very specific areas of journalistic search. For example, the following query:

"putin and berlusconi" ~expert "* said"

…will return results where an expert (or specialist) on the relationship between "putin and berlusconi" has been quoted in a news source (or elsewhere). The * serves as a placeholder for the hypothetical surname of the expert in question (which could be anything), and takes advantage of the journalistic convention of ending quotations with the expression 'so-and-so said'.

Numrange (..): It is possible to force Google to bring back numerical results from a range, using the *numrange* function (two dots placed, without spaces, between two numbers). So:

terrorism 1972..1977

…should (in theory) bring back results about terrorism during the mid-1970s. However, this operator tends to conflate numbers from different areas of the same page which can badly skew results. This function does not appear to recognise symbols (i.e. £), so is best used on raw numbers, rather than values. It may be said that this function is better suited to commercial rather than informational searches.

Domain function (site:): The domain function can be used to refine your search to a particular domain, a type of domain, or a sub-domain in a website. It has many uses – here follow just some.

This function can be used to find expert academics, in a three-stage process, requiring:

Subject terms to cover expertise,

A term connecting the subject to his/her profession (i.e. *expert, department, professor* etc.) and

The domain function: *site:.edu* (filtering results to pages from US universities)

Using this method to find a US expert in solvent abuse might result in a search query like this:

"solvent abuse" professor site:.edu

Where American universities have *.edu* domains, UK universities tend to have *.ac.uk* ones. For other countries around the world, conventions vary – New Zealand uses *.ac.nz*, while Australia uses *.edu.au*. Moreover, in some countries there are no conventions at all in this sector. Top-level domains must be approved by the Internet Assigned Numbers Authority (IANA), and Wikipedia contains a full list of top-level domains:

(http://en.wikipedia.org/wiki/List_of_Internet_top-level_domains).

Example: advanced searching experts

While training in BBC online features, I once asked a features journalist to give an example of a story where finding contributors was particularly difficult and time-consuming. She suggested a story about the influence of political spouses, saying it had taken her hours to find an expert on this rather obscure field. I talked through the above method, and found the same expert she had, in the first result (in less than three minutes), by searching for:

"political spouses" professor site:.edu

Another possible use for the domain function is for finding non-profit groups, or NGOs. These groups often have a *.org* (or in the UK, *.org.uk*) upper-level domain. So the following search:

aberdeen drugs site:.org.uk

...should help unearth Aberdeen-based drug charities, by means of which you might get in touch with experts and professionals (while avoiding references to Aberdeen in Washington, in the US).

But the domain function can also be used to exploit naming convention in web design, towards finding certain types of contributor. For example, WordPress blog accounts (and many websites) feature an *about* folder by default, for profiles, while Blogger accounts feature a *profile* folder. So, for example, by searching for...

> *"climate scientist" site:.com/about*

...you may more accurately find experts in climate science who blog, or who have websites. In addition, finding conversations on Facebook can be done by exploiting the */topic* folder used within the forum section of the site. So:

> *CNN site:facebook.com/topic*

...will return conversations about CNN, which can be useful in terms of reputation management, or newsgathering. This cannot be done using Facebook's search interface.

This function can also be used negatively in order to find content about a topic, but from anywhere other than a particular online source. So if you are a media correspondent, interested in news about The Australian, but not published on The Australian's website, you could try:

> *"the australian" -site:theaustralian.com.au/*

Searching within title (intitle:/allintitle:): This function lets you refine by terms found in the title of a web page. In Search Engine Optimisation, it is widely held that the words entered into a title field in a web page are weighed as highly significant when it comes to determining the 'relevance' of this page in search. By taking advantage of this widely acknowledged convention it is possible to refine your search. Most online news organisations provide backgrounders on big news stories and themes, and they are usually presented (or branded) in a consistent way. So if you want to find background (analysis, not news) on the Somali war in 2007, by taking advantage of the conventions used by some online media, you could try:

> *somalia war intitle:Q&A*

Alternatively, try any of the following keywords: *depth/comment/analysis//brief/background*

Searching within URL (inurl:/allinurl:): This function can be used to find content according to words which appear in the address (i.e. URL or server file path) of a particular web page. So if any type of website may contain your terms, but you do want to find keywords considered 'important' to a particular topic, this can be useful. This function can be used as an alternative to the domain function where search is concerned more with words in the folder structure than words in the domain name. If you are searching for news, then *inurl:* can in practice serve as a very similar function to *intitle:*, insofar as modern news content management systems often generate unique URLs by using keywords from the headline and/or story in question. But for finding content on other, less changeable sites, it serves a unique purpose.

Searching by file (filetype:): There are many reasons why it can be useful to filter your search by the type of file you imagine may contain the information you are looking for. For example, government and corporate reports are often published in PDF format, for ease of printing (these documents are most often read and acted upon not online, but offline). Alternatively, if you are concerned with finding a specialist or expert, it makes sense to confine your search to Powerpoint slides, insofar as experts often present to conferences, and subsequently make these presentations available online. Statistics are often published in Excel (.xls) format, so if you are interested in finding out what were house prices like in Toronto in 2007, the following search will filter out all of those estate agent websites:

"house prices" toronto 2007 filetype:xls

Google will only index the 'rendered' (visible) view of a file, so key metadata which might help identify an author of a file is not necessarily indexed – you have to download the file to check it for yourself. As a good alternative to searching by filetype, there are a range of search verticals which deal exclusively in certain types of media, such as Slideshare (www.slideshare.net), which is concerned with presentations, and Docstoc (www.docstoc.com), which is concerned with sharing text documents.

The language filter: For some types of search it is necessary to omit search results in foreign languages – however those factors used in contextual reference (including Internet Protocol recognition, and language) often render this issue much less of a problem than once it was.

Search in anchor text (inanchor:): Depending on the naming conventions and care with which a website has been constructed, it may be useful to refine a search by concentrating on those words used to embed hyperlinks. Web developers looking to maximise their ranking on Google will use rich, descriptive keywords in their links rather than generic ones – but, of course, the person who uploaded the information you are looking for will not always necessarily be an expert in the field, which is why this function may be of less value than others.

Proximity search (AROUND:): Google has a little-known proximity search function, which allows you to specify, where you are searching for two words, that they appear within a certain number of words of each other. It exploits the principle that words which appear closer together in text are more likely to be connected to each other – and where you are searching for names, this can be a useful way to weed out passing references. It also gives more control over search than the wildcard option. So, for example, if you were doing some research on former French President Nicolas Sarkozy (about his time as president, rather than what he is up to now), you might try:

president AROUND(2) "sarkozy"

Cached pages (cache:): When search engines index web pages, they often take a snap shot image of the page (if the creator of the page permits them to). These 'cached' results often appear within search results next to the web address of the page. They can be essential in seeking out relevant results, as pages can be removed, altered or otherwise compromised in the time between indexing and being returned in your search, and the cache is the only way to get to the information you searched for. Cached pages can be particularly useful in breaking news situations, where online content is removed suddenly. It is not so useful for investigating what sites looked like months, or even years ago – The Internet Archive (http://www.archive.org/index.php), covered in Chapter 6, is a better option in this instance.

Similar pages (related:): If you find a website that is particularly useful to you, you may want to check to see if there are any other sites out there which are similar. If you employ the *related:* function on a web address:

related:irishtimes.com/

Google will use co-citation to present you with as many as 30 'similar' sites to the one you have found. It should be noted again, though, that this is a quantitative measure of similarity, not a qualitative one.

Combining operators

While each of these operators has its own particular use, the real value in advanced searching comes when combinations of operators are used on a particular search problem. There are far too many combinations to list, but here follows a few examples of what is possible.

If you wanted to find out what guidance is being given to help combat sectarianism (sectarian habits, or sectarian behaviour, for example) in New Zealand schools, then try:

*site:.ac.nz OR site:.school.nz "sectarian * schools" ~guide*

If you needed to find a list of (current or former) advisors to Northern Ireland's Ulster Unionist party, try:

"ulster unionist party" advisor site:linkedin.com intitle:United Kingdom

If you were investigating the oil industry in Azerbaijan, and you were looking to find potential whistleblowers, try looking at different companies:

bp OR shell azerbaijan site:linkedin.com/

If you were looking to track details of US arms contracts worth between 20 and 25 million pounds, try:

site:.gov missiles 20M..25M

If you needed to find a contributor who has previously worked at Ikea try:

"ikea" intitle:"curriculum vitae" OR intitle:cv

In each case you should bear in mind that Google indexes lots of different types of information in lots of different formats – and for this reason distortion is often a problem. But by refining you should be able to get closer to your search need. Bear in mind too that some advanced functions can be used negatively.

Remember that all Google advanced operators share the same basic syntax, namely:

operator:search_term

There should be no spaces between operator, colon or search term, failing which your operators will be treated as a search term. Operators can generally be used in conjunction with each other, and with Boolean operators and special characters, but the ALL operators can be problematic.

Search result filters

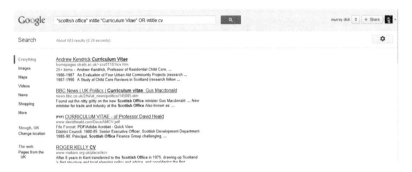

Google's advanced search filters (left-hand column)

The process of refining your search is made easier because Google provides a range of filters on the left-hand side of search results – allowing you to filter by type of source (whether it be images, or forum discussions), by date-range (particularly useful for when time scale is crucial to your research) and by place (you can over-ride the automatic location setting Google selects for you, based on your IP address).

Google's predictive search (Google Instant) can be useful insofar as it can shed light on those areas of the web, prompting keywords and areas of study you may not have thought of before starting your research. Alternatively it can get irritating, and can be switched off within the settings section (wherein, so long as you disable Google Instant, you can specify how many results are returned per page).

In addition to offering refinement by media-type, Google offers a range of other interesting filters which can be useful, and which are often hidden under *More search tools*. It is possible to filter by *Language level*, whereby the words used on the documents returned are analysed, with those pages which contain rarer words are differentiated from those documents which contain more commonly found words. Google's *Timeline* option can also help with some types of search, but only where date of web publication is significant to research. The

Nearby and *Custom location* options can also be very helpful in ironing out differences in meaning across location. A search for 'Ospreys' (the name of a Rugby team) in Swansea will return very different results to the same search done in New York – take advantage of 'local knowledge' as expressed in the words of a locality by changing your location.

The web Pages from the UK	**ROGER KELLY CV** www.makers.org.uk/place/rkcv After 8 years in Kent transferred to the **Scottish Office** in 1975, drawing up Scotland 's first structure and local planning policy and advice, and considering the first ...
Any time Past hour Past 24 hours Past week Past month Past year Custom range...	cardross :: director's cv www.cardrossam.co.uk/cv.htm GE Real Estate & Haslemere Estates Management Ltd - **Scottish Office**. (4/6/00-31/12/04). Senior Portfolio Manager. Responsible for the development ... [PDF] Neal Geaughan's newest CV [CV] www.abdn.ac.uk/business/cv/acc098 File Format: PDF/Adobe Acrobat - Quick View 1985-90, Principal, **Scottish Office** Finance Group, challenging, assessing and advising on proposals for public expenditure, in industry, transport and related ...
All results Sites with images Related searches Dictionary Reading level Social Translated foreign pages Verbatim Fewer search tools	[PDF] **CURRICULUM VITAE** Name: JA (Fred) Coalter Academic ... www.psi.org.uk/pdf/FredCoalterCV.pdf File Format: PDF/Adobe Acrobat - Quick View **Scottish Office**, 1992. The Impact of Concessionary Access Schemes in Leisure. The Association of Directors of Recreation, Leisure and Tourism, 1993 ... [PDF] James Carter cv www.jamescarter.cc/files/jccv.pdf File Format: PDF/Adobe Acrobat - Quick View As manager of the CEI's **Scottish office**, I was responsible for all aspects of the Centre's operations in Scotland. This included securing and managing grant aid, ... [PDF] Leigh Sparks Mini CV April 2011 www.management.stir.ac.uk/people/school-staff/?a=26123 File Format: PDF/Adobe Acrobat - Quick View

Google's advanced filters continued (left-hand column)

Using the Find option to browse a long web page

When it comes to web search – perhaps the most useful utility you will find on your browser is the *Find* utility, available from the Edit menu on your browser, or by pressing the <Control> and F keys at the same time. This lets you cut a dash through reams of information on long, textual pages – and can save you a great deal of time in the process.

Advanced searching Bing

While Bing is Google's main rival for search traffic in the UK, it is, and has been for some time, a long way behind in terms of market share.

Nevertheless, and despite accusations that Bing have been guilty of copying Google (Sullivan, 2011), Bing's index is sufficiently different to make it an important addition to any journalists search tool-kit. Several advanced operators are worthy of note, so here follow some highlights.

Pages containing files (contains:): This operator can be used to find web pages which contain particular file types, rather than the just files. This is a significant improvement on Google's *filetype:* operator insofar as web authors can be remiss in terms of how they name and label their files. Web pages give authors far more scope with which to define, describe and contextualise the files they are sharing. So...

apiculture contains:ppt

...will find pages that contain the word 'apiculture' and have links to files with the *.ppt* extension. Some of the other file types you can search for using this method include *doc, pdf, ppt, rtf, txt* and *xls*.

Proximity search (near:): Bing has a proximity operator which can be used in a similar way to Google's AROUND function:

expert near:3 "chinese politics"

...will find you a range of experts (it is worth noting that Bing will alternate the order of these two expressions).

Co-citation (LinkFromDomain:): this operator identifies the outgoing links from a specific domain, which in turn lets you build a profile of any site you wish to investigate. This operator does not work on all sites.

Availability of Really Simple Synidcation (RSS) feeds (HasFeed:): this operator specifies that any page retrieved which contains your search terms must include a link to an RSS feed. It does not search within the content of RSS feeds, it only returns web pages which contain them. Advanced operators in Bing are employed with the same syntax as it is found in Google.

Advanced searching – some other major search engines

Yahoo (http://uk.yahoo.com/) may be some way behind even Bing in UK search share, but it is nevertheless a major, international search engine. However, while once Yahoo boasted a number of highly useful advanced operators and filters (such as the *region:* operator which allowed searching for content by geography) these are mostly gone now, leaving only a handful of key metasearch options (http://help.yahoo.com/l/us/yahoo/search/basics/basics-04.html).

Ask (http://uk.ask.com/) is another alternative, but like Yahoo it lacks much in the way of innovation, and indeed it has outsourced much of its web crawling to Google, seeking to become a question and answer specialist (Sullivan, 2011). Nevertheless it can be important to use all of these search engines, especially for hard-to-find material. The domain function in both Yahoo and Ask is the same as is found in Google – *site:*.

Exalead (http://www.exalead.com/search/) is a French-based engine, incorporating a number of advanced options which are unavailable in most conventional web search engines, such as phonetic searching, word adjacency and word frequency searching, all available within a user-friendly drop-down on clicking the Advanced search button. This last option is particularly useful for finding background on issues and people.

Metasearch engines

Metasearch engines (or metacrawlers, or federated search engines) are devices which can be used to scour the indexes of several search engines simultaneously. They are often found in commerce (where comparisons are crucial to getting best value), but they are available in general-ist fields too. Some search the most popular engines in a given field, others the most obscure, some present results by source (engine), others present all results cumulatively, using an internal relevance ranking. Advanced search in these tools is determined by the extent to which all of the engines searched share advanced search syntax.

Dogpile (http://dogpile.co.uk/) allows you to find results from Google, Yahoo and Bing, and is a great one-stop-shop for a very broad overview of search results. The engine provides its own form of rele-vance, and lists clearly which engines each result was returned from. There are some limitations in using this engine; there are no cached options, advanced search is limited to Boolean operators, language and domain options, and the sources available from within the news verti-cal are weighted towards US sources and content. Similar to Dogpile are Webcrawler (http://www.webcrawler.com/) and Metacrawler (http://www.metacrawler.com/) (the caveats about searching in Dogpile apply equally to both of these).

Yippy (http://search.yippy.com/) (which used to called Clusty) repre-sents a genuine alternative to all of the above. Its preferences allow the user to set up bespoke tabs from a menu of options (covering web, news and blog verticals), though with the News options spanning CNN,

Reuters, Yahoo! News and NY Times, there is a major US-bias in this engine. Results are easier to interpret thanks to the clustering option, which allows you to refine your search by 'sites' (at the top level this includes domain type, but further down you can refine by particular site). Domain type includes .co.uk which can be used as a loose proxy for UK sites.

Kartoo (http://www.kartoo.com/) is another metasearch engine that presents results using its own relevancy criteria. The designers of this engine opted for clustered results rather than offering advanced operators – and those clusters of results include several which hint at the consumer-driven nature of the engine. Each page in the Kartoo results has its own ranking profile, albeit it may be worth mentioning that Kartoo has no information on a sizable number of sites. This engine is relatively weak when it comes to finding UK people and names, with mis-ordered US name results often out-ranking UK results.

search.com (http://www.search.com/) provides a federated search across Google, Ask, MSN and public directory DMOZ results. Its advanced search features appear, at first glance, to offer a good range of options which all other metasearch engines fail to match, but the language, file-type, domain, link and related options all seem to be drawn exclusively from Google results (and not the others). The Images vertical draws its results form Webshots and Flickr, but results can be limited to just these two sources (it is rare indeed for searches in Google images to result in no results, but not necessarily so in search.com).

One metasearch engine which offers minimalistic search experience with greater reach than virtually all of the above, is Forelook (http://www.forelook.com/), albeit this engine offers less reliability. Zuula (http://www.zuula.com/) does not blend search results from different engines, but rather lets you select which engines to search from a tabbed menu – though there is no way to specify location, and results are US-led. Lastly, ixquick UK (http://ixquick.com/uk/), which claims not to track your IP address, represents a UK-biased alternative to all of the above.

Building your own search engine

Google custom search (www.google.co.uk/cse/) allows you to build customised search engines using its index, which for some specialisms can be a useful way to save time and effort. Simply by collecting a range of domains together, it is possible to search more precisely, and avoid information overload. Alternatively, Rollyo (http://www.rollyo.com/) lets you create your own customised search from Yahoo's index. It used to be possible to pull results together from both engines together into a build-your-own metasearch service (via an online tool called Agent 55), but this is no longer available. Nevertheless, just because you cannot view results from both in one place does not negate the value in searching each individually.

Semantic search

Most traditional search engines used to take a rudimentary, some may say 'dumb' approach to the content they index. Large swathes of information would be indexed, and surfers would search through it, but the engines would not 'understand' what the searcher was looking for, any more than it understood words as strings containing a series of characters. Today all major search engines make great efforts to try to determine what searchers 'mean' by the terms they search for, by interpreting the search terms searchers use, and by differentiating indexed words according to context (like a thesaurus does). This process has been referred to as *semantic search*.

While vestiges of *semantic search* are incorporated into mainstream search, it is equally possible to obtain a purer form of semantic search, by using any of the following engines.

Hakia (http://www.hakia.com/) would more fairly be described as a search portal than a search engine. Semantic search engines often involve natural language queries, rather than keyword search, so advanced operators are not always necessary. If you search Hakia for the expression:

> *what was 'The People's Charter'?*

...the engine should return results which recognise the tense of the question, and can differentiate 'The People's Charter' from other political tracts described in this way. Search results for complex searches like these in Hakia are often comparable with, if not better than Google results.

DuckDuckGo (http://duckduckgo.com/) is another engine which places a high premium on quality in search results. While it has its own self-generated content pages, its main focus is on crowdsourced areas of the web. The site has its own unique and detailed syntax for performing functions (like working out numerical conversions) and advanced one-click searching in certain popular domains (e.g. *!bbc "prince william"* will search the BBC index for stories about Prince William).

Self-styled 'Web 3.0 search engine' Kngine (http://www.kngine. com/) offers an alternative, albeit rather US-centric, option. They also offer a statistics vertical, drawing exclusively upon UN, World Bank,

CIA Factbook and other official material. If you needed to find out adult literacy levels in Belgium, then it might make sense to start here rather than with a generic search engine.

Visual search

Most search engine developers recognised long ago that the 10-links-on-a-page format of search results is an unsustainable way of dealing with the ever-growing volume of information on the Web. For this reason, there is today a wide range of visual search engines, whose results are presented in a more intuitive way. Sometimes this is an aesthetic measure, aimed at muting the volume of results, but for other engines the visual nature of search results makes for a different search experience, whereby the surfer can gain new insights into search results.

Visual search engine NewsMap, which exploits the Google News API
Source: Newsmap, by Marcos Weskamp. http://newsmap.jp.

NewsMap (http://newsmap.jp) is probably the best place to go on the net for a visual overview of key stories of the day, as drawn from the index of Google News. News stories are presented as a treemap visualisation. This site offers some versatility when it comes to coverage selection; you can include or leave out world news, and other topical areas. The size of each cell reflects the volume of related articles found in Google News story clusters around these themes, so in essence it gives you an insight into the dominant news values of different groups of media. This site is as close as it is possible to be to a round-up in one place, from a good selection of news sources (and it is reasonably up-to-date, albeit not strictly speaking real-time).

Quintura (http://www.quintura.com/) is a long-established, and much-praised engine in this field. However, for some searches this engine will return borderline-irrelevant content – no doubt due to the fact that it lacks any sense of understanding the meaning in the words which crop up. Nevertheless, the basic technology (and the building-blocks approach to search refinement) serves as a good introduction to the potential in visual search.

Spezify (http://www.spezify.com/) can be useful for visualising information across consumer, social media and multimedia sites (from Amazon, to Twitter, to SoundCloud), providing a mixed palate of information across fields and media-types.

Search cloud (http://www.searchcloud.net/) can be used to weigh the words you want, in terms of their relative frequency, across a set of search results. So, for example, if you were interested in researching the UK cash for peerages scandal of 2006/7, and you were interested in finding reports and material which featured Tony Blair, Lord Levy, Dr Chai Patel and John McTernan, it is possible using Search cloud to 'weight' those terms individually – such that if John McTernan were the key focus of the research, by increasing the size of font in the 'cloud' (relative to the font size for the other search terms), more material should come back which references him more than the others. Unfortunately the site does not give much away about how its underlying technology works, about how re-scaling the size of each term impacts on relevance, nor about where its index comes from, but it nevertheless offers a very different, and innovative alternative to search.

Social search

The term 'social search', or even the application of the term 'social' to the concept of search is conceptually redundant insofar as the ranking methods used in leading engines represent a form of endorsement, and so are inherently social (Halavais, 2009, p. 160). But those developing and using the online tools which fall into this category do not seem to mind.

It has been argued, as an alternative to conventional information retrieval, that human intercession in relevance may go beyond an atomistic search 'need', towards enabling the potential in social capital to solve community problems otherwise conceptualised as 'sociable media' (Donath and Boyd, 2004). But whether this field is conceived as 'sociable media', 'collaborative filtering', 'social search' or 'crowdsourcing', the principal is simple, rather than rely exclusively (or mostly) upon metrics when it comes to determining what is 'relevant' in search, social search engines harness the wisdom (and efforts) of the crowd (or social graph), and communities of interest, to bring relevance to search.

For the purposes of structuring this book, I have differentiated between the process of social search as defined above, and both people finders (many of which are social search engines), social bookmarking sites, and social news sites, all of which are dealt with separately, in later chapters.

blekko: a social search engine on the rise

blekko (http://blekko.com/) represents a radical, social alternative to Google in search – and its developer have come into conflict with big UK online web companies (such as CompareTheMarket.com) over the interpretation, and exclusion of 'spam' from their index (Arthur, 2010). This engine's index is structured around human activity, rather than the spidering of an algorithm. Its approach to search is described as 'slashtag search', which hints at the hierarchical, taxonomical, human-centric nature of organisation used. At present some searches are a little light on content by comparison with its long-established competition. But the social nature of this engine (and its wider recognition at least within the search community) mean that if any product is likely to challenge received wisdom in search, then this may be it.

Scour (http://www.scour.com/) is a composite social/federated search engine. It takes the principal of social news sites (where relevance is determined by people voting up and down the articles they most enjoy or trust), and applies it to results generated by Google, Yahoo!, Bing and OneRiot (as well as using its own ranking). The idea is to develop a community of trust, so taking part in voting (and also commenting on web search results – which often contain partisan posturing rather than insightful analysis) is dependent upon registering for an account with the service. The company clearly hope that surfers will encourage friends to do likewise, and so harness 'relevance' based on real-world communities.

This approach brings into question the efficacy of voting as a measure of *relevance*, in terms of journalistic enquiry. It is unclear, for example, whether people are voting for or against material based on its accuracy, or if they are simply voting content up or down because they *like* (or dislike) particular documents (or authors). Moreover, just because consensus can be reached on a topic does not mean conclusions drawn from this consensus are correct, or accurate. Eurekster's Community Powered Web Search (http://community-powered-web-search-swicki. eurekster.com/) provides an alternative to Scour.

ChaCha (http://www.chacha.com/) attempts to harness the wisdom of its users to answer common questions. The result is something most journalists should be able to appreciate – search for any concept (say presidential election), and results are returned in a who, what, where, when-type format. A more intuitive service, and one based on the very public expertise of its community, is provided by Quora (http://www.quora.com/).

Mobile search

At the time of writing there are few significant alternatives to the major search brands who have carved out a significantly alternative niche in mobile search (not withstanding Siri for Apple iOS, which is more of a personal assistant than a search vertical *per se*). In future, developments in mobile search will likely be driven by geo-location, predictive search and voice-recognition.

Some sources in search

There are many sources online which offer updates on developments in search, here follows a list of the most useful:

Bing Search Blog:
http://www.bing.com/community/blogs/search/

Phil Bradley's Weblog:
http://www.philbradley.typepad.com/

Google Operating Systems (unofficial):
http://googlesystem.blogspot.com/

(Official) Google Blog:
http://googleblog.blogspot.com/

Karen Blakeman's Blog:
http://www.rba.co.uk/wordpress/

LifeHacker:
http://lifehacker.com/

Mashable:
http://mashable.com/

Pandia:
http://www.pandia.com/

Read Write Web:
http://www.readwriteweb.com/

Search Engine Land:
http://searchengineland.com/

Search Engine Watch:
http://searchenginewatch.com/

Tech Crunch:
www.techcrunch.com/

The Next Web:
http://thenextweb.com/

Browser extensions for search

Some highly useful search tools come in the form of browser add-ons
(or extensions), which are small programs run in conjunction with
internet browsers.

Surf Canyon's browser extension (http://www.surfcanyon.com
/extension.jsp), used in conjunction with Firefox, will personalise
results when searching in particular search engines. Likewise, Google's
Similar Pages beta (https://chrome.google.com/extensions), when used
in conjunction with the Chrome browser, will suggest similar pages to
the ones you find.

There are many other extensions available, so it is worthwhile keeping on top of these over time. Here follow the 'big four' browser application directories (the Firefox directory is probably the most active – some
add-ons created for this browser will be re-visited in subsequent chapters in this book).

Chrome extensions directory:
https://chrome.google.com/extensions/?hl=en

Firefox extensions directory:
https://addons.mozilla.org/en-US/firefox/

Microsoft Internet Explorer extensions directory:
http://www.ieaddons.com/gb/

Safari extensions directory:
http://extensions.apple.com/

References

Arthur, Charles (2010) New search engine Blekko labels MoneySavingExpert and CompareTheMarket 'spam', *The Guardian*, November 02: http://www.guardian.co.uk/technology/blog/2010/nov/02/blekko-search-engine-labels-money-sites-spam

BBC (2006) Google Censors itself for China, bbc.co.uk/news, January 25: http://news.bbc.co.uk/1/hi/technology/4645596.stm

Calishain, Tara (2005) *Web Search Garage*. New Jersey: Prentice Hall PTR (Pearson Education, Inc).

Donath, Judith and Boyd , Danah (2004) 'Public Displays of Connection', *BT Technology Journal*, 22(4), 71–82: http://smg.media.mit.edu/papers/Donath/PublicDisplays.pdf

Google (2012) 'Search quality highlights: 50 changes for March', Inside Search (The Official Google Search Blog), April 03: http://insidesearch.blogspot.co.uk/2012/04/search-quality-highlights-50-changes.html

Henninger, Maureen (2008) *The Hidden Web: Finding Quality Information on the Net (2nd Edition)*. UNSW Press: Sidney.

Long, Johnny (2005) *Google Hacking for Penetration Testers*. Syngress Publishing, Inc.

Schlein, Alan M (2004) *Find it Online, The Complete Guide to Online Research (Fourth Edition)*. Arizona: Facts on Demand Press.

Sullivan, Dan (2011) Google: Bing Is Cheating, Copying Our Search Results, Search Engine Land, February 01: http://searchengineland.com/google-bing-is-cheating-copying-our-search-results-62914

Thurow, Shari and Musica, Nick (2009) *When Search Meets Web Usability*. Berkeley: New Riders.

3 The invisible web

Search engines are not the only means of finding information online. Indeed some of the most useful online tools in the journalists' armoury are expressly not available via search engines, because this content does not exist on the *surface web*, where web crawlers can find it. Some research tasks are far better resolved by going straight to source, by finding interactive mediums or sources of expertise beyond the wisdom of the crowd. This is especially true where search tasks are complex, hard to express in simple terms or unlikely to exist in a convenient place online.

The *deep*, *invisible* or *hidden* web, as it has alternatively been called, is a concept which has challenged the web development community since the mid-1990s. Broadly speaking, it is conceptualised as those areas of online material which are non-accessible to general search engines, World Wide Web content which lurks beneath the areas routinely indexed by major search companies. More detailed definitions of this concept have been prone to change over time.

Sherman and Price (2001) offer a thorough overview of what the 'hidden' web contains, and why this content is there:

Type of invisible web content	Why it is invisible
Disconnected page	No links for crawlers to find the page
Page consisting primarily of images, audio or video	Insufficient text for the search engine to 'understand' what the page is about
Pages consisting primarily of PDF or Postscript, Flash, Shockwave, Executables (programs) or Compressed files (.zip, .tar, etc.)	Technically indexable, but usually ignored, primarily for business or policy reasons
Content in relational databases (often created using SQL)l	Crawlers cannot fill out required fields in interactive forms
Real-time content	Ephemeral data; huge quantities; rapidly changing information
Dynamically generated content	Customised content is irrelevant for most searchers; fear of "spider traps"

(Sherman and Price, 2001, p. 61).

In addition to this typology of hidden content, the authors went on to explain the existence of the invisible web by dividing it into four sub-divisions of information. The invisible web is therefore conceived as an umbrella term for:

The Opaque web (files which can be, but are not indexed)
The Private web (deliberately excluded, passwords/robots.txt/ noindex)
The Proprietary web (hidden behind paywalls)
Truly Invisible web (the edge of search engine development)
    (2001, p. 70)

But even back in 2001, it was acknowledged that 'what may be invisible today may become visible tomorrow' (Sherman and Price, 2001, p. 56), due in part to indexing policy, and in part to advances in search engine technology.

In 2008, Henninger refined these early definitions to exclude pass-word-protected content, and content which uses HTML tags to prevent indexing and caching. This definition of the invisible web encapsulated 'publicly accessible, non-proprietary pages that are not "seen" by the spiders of general search engines' (Henninger, 2008, p. 162). Broken down into its constituent forms, this includes *grey literature*, mate-rial not commercially published, or hard to find commercially, such as committee reports, and other official documentation (Henninger, 2008, p. 169).

More recently still, some have questioned the usefulness of the 'invisible web' as a concept (given that a number of research findings used to define it are becoming evermore obsolete, with the passage of time). It has been questioned just how useful ephemeral online infor-mation within the invisible web really is (Ryan, 2008). Equally, content which is now widely accessible in general search engines (indexing policies aside), but which was not when the concept first came to pass, include:

Pages in non-HTML formats (PDF, Word, Excel, PowerPoint) now converted into HTML.
Script-based pages, whose URLs contain a *?* or other script coding.
Pages generated dynamically by other types of database software (e.g. Active Server Pages, Cold Fusion). These can be indexed if there is a stable URL somewhere that search engine crawlers can find.
    (University of California, Berkeley, 2010)

Today Google et al. are trying to solve the invisible web problem by developing technologies which analyse and query databases on the web, whose content has until now been off-bounds, but this is a major project, with the breadth and range of database types available (Wright, 2009).

But whatever current or future definitions of the 'invisible web' we may use, general search may never provide the answers to many research questions. Today it is often far more efficient to go directly to directories, portals (community-driven subject directories), vortals (a portal focussed on one industry), gateway services (subscription resources where specialists help meet research needs) and other alternative search *verticals*.

People finders: subscription and free

Most media organisations have subscriptions to directories for finding people. These are proprietary online databases which combine official public data, such as (in the UK) the edited electoral roll, or directory enquiries, and which often include other sources of people-finding information too.

One of the better known premium sources in this field is 192.com (www.192.com/). This service offers a range of useful data sets, from current (and historic) electoral roll data, through information on directorships, births marriages and deaths, house prices (current and historic) business listings, maps and even company credit reports. Some of this information can be obtained elsewhere, and not all content is premium, such as directory enquires, which can be found freely elsewhere (http://www.thephonebook.bt.com/). However, the availability of all this information in one place makes for a particularly powerful (if relatively expensive) people-finding tool.

The ability to sort results by age-range for some (not all) people makes for a hugely useful filter (especially for common names). An inbuilt thesaurus which looks for contractions of common names, a visualisation option for checking when people have been registered at a particular property, and the option to view by house price, all contribute to improve search strategy. Director reports can also be mined in order to undertake social network analysis on individuals, showing who company directors know, and how far their public influence extends.

Example: follow the money ...

While working in a regional newsroom in South Yorkshire, I was asked if it were possible to find out the associates of a local businessman convicted of fraud online. Using 192.com, we found director reports for his companies, all of which listed co-directors and other affiliates, which the journalists then used to pursue further leads.

As an alternative to 192.com, Tracesmart (www.tracesmart.co.uk/) (also a subscription) offer a different range of specialist tools, in addition to public directories. This service includes a (limited) mobile phone directory and a range of other public records directories (including individual small share holdings). Further premium alternatives to 192.com and Tracesmart, include:

Cameo (http://cameo.bvdep.com/) (electoral roll information only)

GB Accelerator e-Trace (http://www.gb.co.uk/gbgroup/products/gb-accelerator-e-trace-debtor-tracing) (which includes Royal Mail Postcode Address File data).

But it is important to consider one caveat when it comes to these official sources of public information. Since 2003, as a consequence of Data Protection legislation, people have had the right to opt out of many such databases. Moreover, the increasing number of people making their landline numbers ex-directory and opting for mobile telephones as an alternative to landlines contrives to make these *official* methods of people finding less and less useful as time goes on. It has been predicted that landline telephones have less than 15 years of mass use left (Economist, 2009), which may serve as a benchmark for how much longer official people-finders along the lines discussed above may remain useful.

Yet ironically, just as people are asserting their right to privacy by having their names struck off public directories, so too are they voluntarily sharing aspects of their personal lives across the web. Most of the leading search engines do not offer people-finder verticals, so a gap in the market has opened up into which several free people-finding search engine brands have stepped.

123people (http://www.123people.co.uk/) is a free search engine that focuses on indexing those areas of the web most likely to yield information about people, including areas of the hidden web. It then sorts results by *type* of web content (and so images, email addresses and phone numbers are presented separately). Web content on 123people is a composite of Yahoo, MSN and Google results, and media content is organised by format (so Word documents, PDFs and other formats are all distinguished from each other). The tag cloud viewer offers more than merely an interesting representation of results – this way of representing information goes beyond the linear strictures of ten search results, and lets you see which words are most associated with the name you are searching for.

One significant weakness with 123people (as with all free people finders), is the use of 'best match' (as opposed to 'exact match') in search results. The web is not a neatly constructed database with matching content, and easy-to-access, consistent data. So when searching for images, pages containing images of other people (but textual references to the person you searched for) will be returned. When it comes to emails, it is perhaps inevitable, given the various conventions people and companies use in configuring email accounts, that inconsistency abounds. These can include:

firstname.surname@domain
firstinitialsurname@domain
surname.initial@domain

On the other hand, such free people finders do offer something conventional search engines cannot – Google, for example (officially at least) does not index @ signs (Long, 2005).

Pipl (http://pipl.com/) is a popular alternative to 123people. However, Pipl is arguably less helpful when it comes to identifying UK domains (either by registration or upper level domain) than it is when searching for US content. Much content in this database comes from social media sites, with a heavy emphasis on YouTube and Myspace content, all archives (geaneological) and news articles are from US sources (at the time of writing). Pipl encourages you to select a location, but does not let you include keywords in your search, which may help refine results where you are searching for a common name.

Yasni (http://www.yasni.com/) is a German competitor to both 123people and Pipl, which (unlike the other two) offers an email alert service (similar to Google News alerts) for new mentions of a name across the Web over time. Social Register (http://www.socialregister.co.uk/) is another option for people finding online.

In addition to these web-based engines, today there are many mobile application people-finders available, which can be used in breaking news situations to track what is happening in a given place. These include:

BrightKite (http://brightkite.com/)
Buzzd (http://www.buzzd.com/)
Foursquare (account required) (https://foursquare.com/)
Gowalla (http://gowalla.com/)

As an alternative to these free people finders, there are today a range of file-specific search engines, that is to say, engines which let you search for particular types of file, which can in turn help you to find particular types of contributor (such as experts who have produced publications on their specialism). They are not quite equivalent to doing a filetype: search in Google (covered in the previous chapter), insofar as they have their own indexes. They include docstoc (www.docstoc.com/) and Scribd (www.scribd.com/).

If you are searching for US citizens, there are many more people finders which can help including:

iSearch (http://www.isearch.com/)
Intelius (http://www.intelius.com/)
Spokeo (www.spokeo.com/)
PeekYou (www.peekyou.com/)
Wink (www.wink.com/)
Yahoo People Search (http://people.yahoo.com/)

Because of the current unstructured nature of web content, the subscription model of 'official' people-finder will continue to be necessary to marketers, policymakers, credit-checkers, law enforcers and any number of other professions besides journalists. Until the internet contains a higher quotient of meaningful (semantic) information, the current generation of people finders will need to be supplemented.

Example: hidden needles...

Free people finders may lack precision, but they can be useful when combined with other, official sources. While consulting for an NGO, I was asked to find the contact details of a popular (and controversial) public figure. Electoral roll results were misleading – the results returned did not match the individual's social class profile. However, searching for the name in 123people returned an Amazon wish list which indicated that the person in question is known by his substituted middle names. Armed with this hidden knowledge, his identity became clear with subsequent searches of the electoral roll.

Finding local knowledge

When it comes to finding local people, and where they spend their time (as opposed to where they live), then local knowledge is the key. So when seeking out vox pops in an unfamiliar area, The Knowhere Guide (http://www.knowhere.co.uk/) can be useful. The site was set up by skateboarders around the UK, sharing information on places to skate and places to avoid. Today most towns in the UK have a profile on the site. Here you can find out (via the *Hookup Spots* pages) places to go and places not to go to meet people, while the 'Cringing Cult of Celebrity' section tells you of famous sons and daughters in the area (much like Wikipedia's entries for towns do, albeit these are probably less reliable). There is no Wiki system of authority on this site, so every fact found here will require verification (as should any other piece of information you find online).

Finding experts

Perhaps the easiest means of finding experts is to search for expertise within search verticals covering books and literature, which would include Amazon and Google Books. Amazon permits browsing by topic, and results filtering by both popularity (one way of establishing authority in some – though not all, fields) and date of publication (which can be used to find relevant forthcoming releases – some releases in Amazon are years ahead of publication).

As an alternative to such mainstream book verticals, Abe Books may help with more obscure specialisms, albeit (obviously) the longer a book has been out of print, the less likely the author will be around to field your call. Other options in literature verticals include:

Biblio (http://www.biblio.com/)
Google Books (http://books.google.com/)
Library thing (http://www.librarything.com/)
What Should I Read Next (http://www.whatshouldireadnext.com/)

For a more tailored experience, Profnet (https://profnet.prnewswire.com/) has been used by UK journalists as a means of sourcing PR, expertise and case studies since 1992. Free to journalists (but not the 'experts' whose details are indexed), it helps with most sourcing problems, though of course ultimately, there is no guarantee that the experts are comfortable in front of a camera or with a microphone under their nose. It could equally be argued that this is altogether a too convenient way to source expertise, and that it risks limiting public opinion in news coverage to the contents or a relatively tiny sample of the population. When used in conjunction with the search strategies outlined in the previous chapter, however, it makes a valuable contribution towards newsgathering.

For legal expertise, Sweet and Maxwell's Legal Hub (http://www. legalhub.co.uk/) contains a Bar Directory for sourcing lawyers and an Expert Witness directory. For an alternative to the Bar Directory, Lawyer Locator (http://www.lawyerlocator.co.uk/) can be helpful.

Finding academics

There are number of ways to find scientific expertise online. For news-gathering purposes, specialist research outlets like Alphagalileo (http://www.alphagalileo.org/) and Eurekalert (http://www.eurekalert.org/) can prove fruitful. Alternatively, Google Scholar is near equivalent to the expensive academic resources universities subscribe to. Google Scholar search results are ordered by volume of citations by default, which is one way to measure authority – the peer review process in academia is (it could be argued) a more reliable way of measuring this than the volume of sales. Google Scholar offers email alerts.

Finding contributors via charities

Finding contributors for some social issues can be fraught with ethical dilemmas. In the first instance, it is probably best to approach people with sensitive conditions through the organisations they come into regular contact with, rather than contacting them directly. Asking a charity, care group or other NGO to circulate a request for contributions is more likely to yield positive results, and less likely to end with potential interviewees feeling harassed.

For 'issues-based' stories, for example, health or social issues, poverty or social mobility, AskCharity (http://www.askcharity.org.uk/) contains a detailed directory of charities likely to yield both experts (such as practitioners and professionals in certain fields) and those who have experience of the issue at hand (who have come into contact with practitioners). The site offers journalists a case study mass mail-out to all relevant organisations in its index (though this is expressly not for the use of student journalists). For an alternative, browsable index of charities and activist groups on several alternative issues, see the contacts and links database in Schnews (http://www.schnews.org.uk/ links/index.php).

While for the most part the Charity Commission website (http:// www.charity-commission.gov.uk/) was established to monitor NGOs' financial details, it can also be used to keyword search groups working in fields which are unfamiliar to you. For example, Policy Library's site (http://www.policylibrary.com/) contains many think tanks, research centres and policy workers, papers, research and press releases from around the world. Equally, the National Council for Voluntary Organisations (http://www.charity-commission.gov.uk/) have significant news section, where campaigns at national and local levels are publicised. Internationally, the Worldwide NGO directory is a more fitting source (http://www.wango.org/resources.aspx?section=ngodir).

Finding celebrities

Spotlight (http://www.spotlight.com/) is the industry standard subscription database for finding actors and actresses (and child actors), albeit not all are by any means 'celebrities'. There is an element of quality control in this long-standing subscription-based brand, everyone herein must be professionally trained or experienced performers. A free-to-use alternative to this model is available in the form of Casting Call Pro (www.uk.castingcallpro.com/).

If you cannot afford subscriptions to Celebrities Worldwide (www. celebritiesworldwide.com/) or Who's Who (www.ukwhoswho.com/), there are some free (albeit less reliable) alternatives. Most of the bigger acting agents have their own websites, and indexed directories.

Finding people via news archives

While some in academe have raised concerns about the lack of pluralism involved in the way journalists return again and again to the same sources, using the media to source contributors for some stories can nevertheless be essential. For example, if FIFA were to issue a new safety procedure covering football stadia, you may want to speak to someone who has lived through a disaster at a football stadium to substantiate your piece. But if you cannot find anything in your own newspaper's archive, you may dig through a newspaper's archive, and find the names (and most likely ages – journalistic convention should see to that) of those who have been affected. Once you have these, you can take your details to a people-finding directory like 192.com and check using their age-profiling option.

Nexis and subscription newspaper archives

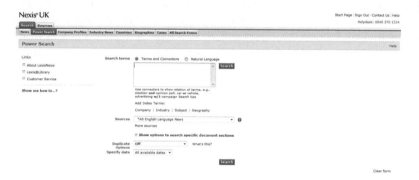

Nexis: newspaper archives are a fairly reliable way to source information online

Nexis is a newspaper cuttings database whose archives go (for the most part) back to the early-mid 1990s, and in some cases further still. It is an enormous repository of news archives, designed and developed long before the user-friendly and intuitive search experience we (mostly) associate with current-state search engines. As such, the unfamiliar must come to terms with a different kind of search experience when trying to get the best out of Nexis. Though studies suggest that the service may be lacking in the archival of wires (press agency) copy (Weaver and Bimber, 2008), it is nevertheless one of the most popular (and regularly used) tool available to journalists in their research.

An easy way into Nexis is to go for the *Power Search* option (see the left-hand column). At the top of the page you will see a Simple Search box. Note the radio buttons for *Terms and connectors* and *Natural Language*. The default is set to the former, which allows you to add search functions, which will give you more control over your searching than merely using natural language.

The sheer volume of content in Nexis puts a premium on refining, and because all information is in a common format (i.e. news articles, with common fields); it is possible to provide some very specific field operators, which can significantly speed up search. Here are selections of some of the most useful ones:

AND: you have to put this between all terms and connectors (Google allows spaces, Nexis does not).

OR: if you want to return results containing one or other term, use this.

AND NOT: use this to remove results containing words you definitely do not want (though be wary of false positives).

ATLEAST8(): this function allows you to set a threshold (i.e. 8) for the frequency with which your terms appear in results. If you are looking for an interview with an individual, or for a backgrounder for an issue, use this to refine your results, and miss out all the passing references. Use the function on the person's surname, then include a phrase search for their full name – i.e. *ATLEAST5(cameron) AND "david cameron"*.

LENGTH>(): This operator allows you to return results either above (>) or below (<) a certain word-length. This is useful for finding depth articles – few analyses of any major issue would be less than 800–900 words, so you can miss out all those news in briefs.

BYLINE(): If you work in a particular beat, and want to find out if one of your competitors has written something on an issue before, use this function to pull back all their work. Alternatively, use the **SECTION()** function.

HEADLINE(): this operator provides a very restrictive search, when you are getting too many results, and other filters are not helping you.

Once you have decided what terms and operators to use (usually an iterative process), you can then determine which papers (or groups of papers) to search, and the time-span you want to search within. Here follows a series of examples showing how to use these operators together, where you want to find some detailed background information about the **G20**, with sources set to *UK Broadsheets*, and time-span set to *previous five years*.

A search for: *G20*... returned >3000 results.

This search returns too many results, even when changing the ranking to relevance. We can filter out passing references to G20, and increase the relevance of these results by using the ATLEAST function.

A search for: *ATLEAST7(G20)*... returned <200 results.

This search is getting much more accurate, but there are still too many stories to read in ten minutes, to get a backgrounder on this organisation.

It is possible to filter out those short stories which clog up the 'relevance' results ranking, and so focus on the lengthy pieces which feature the term G20 at least seven times.

A search for: *ATLEAST7(G20)* AND LENGTH(>1000)...returned <100 results.

This is another improvement, but not enough. If references to Gordon Brown were important to this search, the following string would suffice:

A search for: *ATLEAST7(G20) AND "gordon brown" AND LENGTH(>1000)*...returned <60 results.

The results are refined, but it is possible to specify another very restrictive filter on this search – that all results coming back must feature G20 in the headline (this includes standfirsts):

A search for: *ATLEAST7(G20) AND "gordon brown" AND LENGTH (>1000) AND HEADLINE(G20)*...returned <50 results.

Working through these advanced options allows search refinement to the point where a manageable number of results is returned. But in addition, when results are returned, they can also be sorted by *relevance* (see the drop down on the top-left) which can help to speed the process. Finally, all of these articles can be saved as a text or Word file. Nexis can also be used to generate original features ideas, depending on timing. By searching for at least five mentions of the keyword 'alcohol', within the *Society, Social Welfare and Lifestyle* subject, for articles written more than ten years ago, for example, it is possible to harvest some features ideas which may merit re-visiting, ten years later.

While archive search is often associated with the past, it can also be put to good use for finding upcoming events too, by searching the past few days' or weeks' content in the archive. Try using something like:

"home office" AND "next week" OR "next month"

As an alternative to Nexis, Factiva (http://www.dowjones.com/factiva/index.asp) offers a similar (subscription) service, and similarly useful advanced operators, much like those available in Nexis. These include *same* for finding two terms in the same paragraph, *w/n* for finding one word within a certain number of words (n) of another word, or *near/n* for finding one word within a certain number of words (n) of another word, where they appear in any order in the text.

Example: don't Sam so close to me...

Proximity search can be particularly useful when seeking out connections between people. When training a Sports journalist, I was asked to find context on the relationship between former Newcastle Football Club manager Sam Allardyce, and Manager of Manchester United, Alex Ferguson. A search in Factiva (subscription) for:

"sam allardyce" near "alex ferguson"

...brought back a court report in a local paper about a lawyer who stole from a paralysed man. Hidden at the bottom of the article it was mentioned in passing, that the accused 'was a member of the prestgious (sic) Mere Golf and Country Club where regulars include football managers Sir Alex Ferguson, Sam Allardyce'. While this information might be useless in and of itself, it could be useful for anyone trying to contextualise comments made by either manager about the other in the press (i.e. supportive remarks). It highlights what interesting pieces of information can be teased out of online search, which would be massively time-consuming using basic free-text.

As for web-based alternatives to Nexis and Factiva, which anyone can access, there are further alternatives:

The British Newspaper Archive (http://www.britishnewspaperarchive.co.uk/)
Google News Archive (http://news.google.co.uk/archivesearch)
HighBeam (http://www.highbeam.com/)

Legal resources

Whether you need to consult legislation or to keep track of who is appearing in court in the next few days, there are a handful of essential tools available in the UK, including:

Bailli (http://www.bailii.org/rss/): free updates on UK and Irish case law and legislation (includes RSS feeds).
Courtserve (http://www.courtserve.net/): subscription for up-to-date cases at Royal, Crown and County courts, as well as Scottish and Welsh courts, and UK Tribunals.
HM Courts (http://www.hmcourts-service.gov.uk/): for forthcoming court lists and judgements.

Legislation for all UK Acts of Parliament, by jurisdiction (http://www.
legislation.gov.uk/).

Outlaw (http://www.out-law.com/page-0): free legal guidance on
technological issues (by Pinsent and Mason).

Scottish Courts (http://www.scotcourts.gov.uk/): for forthcoming
court lists and judgements.

Westlaw (http://www.westlaw.co.uk/): subscription for finding cases,
among other things.

Financial search tools

Sometimes it is helpful to look up an individual's business records to
give insight into their character, or something you have heard about
them. Here follows several UK financial sources which help shed light
on the business goings on of individuals, and corporations:

Companies House (http://www.companieshouse.gov.uk/): subscription for all official public company documentation, which includes
disallowed director information free.

Corporate Data (www.corporateinformation.com): subscription
which includes a decade of earnings information.

Credit Safe (http://creditsafeuk.com/): subscription for credit checks:
you need permission of the person you are searching, according to
the Data Protection Act 1998.

Director Check (http://company-director-check.co.uk/): find companies by director.

Individual Insolvency Register Search (http://www.insolvency.gov.
uk/eiir/).

Level Business (http://www.levelbusiness.com/): free company report
and accounts.

London Stock Exchange (https://www.londonstockexchange.com/):
offers email alerts for breaking news on company matter.

Land Registry (www.landregistryservice.co.uk/Ownership): subscription
useful for finding out who owns a property (by title, plan or lease).

Orbis (Bureau Van Dijk) (https://orbis.bvdep.com/ip/): subscription
covering key data for companies operating around the world.
Includes corporate structures, which can be useful when investigating international corporate relationships.

Red Flag Alert (http://www.redflagalert.com/): subscription which, in
addition to company information, includes a unique 'alert' measurement of company 'health'.

Registry Trust (http://www.trustonline.org.uk/): details of County Court judgements.

Scoot (http://www.scoot.co.uk/): business directory, like Yellow Pages.

SCoRe (Search Company Reports) (http://www.score.ac.uk/): integrated search covering various UK collections of historical company reports. Useful when searching for past connections between companies.

Search Systems UK (http://publicrecords.searchsystems.net/): exhaustive list of subscription services covering everything from Aircraft registrations to World War II warships – includes many rare databases.

UK Data: company credit reports (http://www.ukdata.com).

Finding people by their family history

When it was discovered in 2010 that Ed Miliband is not named on his eldest child's birth certificate, this became front-page news for the *Daily Mail*. This story is evidence of the potential in ancestry databases for sourcing news. Here are some key UK sources in this field:

Ancestry.co.uk (http://www.ancestry.co.uk/): subscription, for all family tree, genealogy and census records, includes data sets on births marriages and deaths, census, migration, military records.

Find My Past (http://www.findmypast.co.uk/): competitor service to Ancestry.co.uk.

National Archives (http://www.nationalarchives.gov.uk/documentsonline/): provides databases from many sources of public and state information, from air force records to wills. You will need to visit the archives in Kew to access some online tools.

Your local public library

Many of us are used to borrowing books, CDs, DVDs, and even drinking frothy coffee in local public libraries. But some UK local library authorities provide other services which are especially useful in journalistic research. Some of Greater London's borough libraries, among others across the country, provide access to highly useful online subscription resources. To access these sources from home, you need a library card number and (sometimes) an electronic pin number for the library authority that subscribes.

NewsUK and Newsbank

For those who cannot afford subscription news archives, there are free alternatives available at your local library. Although the search functions are pretty crude (and limiting) by comparison with Nexis and Factiva, NewsUK (www.newsuk.co.uk/) and Newsbank (www.newsbank.com/) offer phrase searching, date spans, a broad range (and depth) of regional and national titles, and the option to sort results by relevance (whereby those articles which feature your terms most frequently appear upper-most in your search results).

KnowUK

KnowUK (www.knowuk.com/) is a subscription 'meta-search engine', allowing users to search across more than 100 reference sources, many of which contain information not freely available over the net. For ease and convenience, the databases in KnowUK are organised into categories on the left-hand navigation. Because its uses are so many and so diffuse, here follows just some of the more useful categories for journalists.

Biography offers 20 biographical databases, which include generic sources (Debrette's and Who's Who for finding 'the great and good'), political sources (a database for each governmental body in UK politics), through clerical, civil service, sporting and even obituaries sources. Most of these sources include information such as work and life history, as well as hobbies and even sometimes contact details. As such they can be put to a number of uses.

Example: shark sandwich...

While training two natural history researchers, I was asked if it were possible to find a celebrity (for a pilot) who has a genuine interest in sharks. Take such a request to a castings agency, you may likely be sent anyone, but if you search through the biographical databases found in KnowUK you will find that Lloyd Grossman is a patron of the Shark Trust, and a PADI-certified divemaster. You will also learn that Francis Rossi lists Coy Carp as a pass-time, and that Elaine Paige is a keen clay pigeon shooter.

As for the parliamentary databases, these include lots of useful information about MPs, such as their majority at the last election, their career history, membership of committees, their political interest, their commercial interests and contact details. These are therefore useful contacts databases for any budding political journalist looking for a political contributor. House of Commons Biographies (published by Dods), European Parliamentary Biographies, House of Lords Biographies, Scottish Parliamentary Biographies and Welsh Assembly Biographies cover each legislature by degrees.

If you are working on a story about a local school, search to see if any MPs or other public figures attended it, they may provide some colourful actuality. House of Commons Biographies even includes former professions. Alternatively, if your MP is active on Twitter, you will find them on Tweetminster (http://tweetminster.co.uk/mps/search), but if not, there are alternatives such as the Urban75 list (http://www.urban75.com/Action/politicians.html).

Events contains forward planning resources. It can be used to search by keyword or location for events coming up for the year, and perhaps most usefully it can be searched by category.

General Knowledge contains some useful statistical sources in the form of Regional and Social Trends, in an easily searchable format (unlike the ONS site, which can be difficult at times). Also see Titles and Forms of Address, which helps to avoid faux pas when addressing the landed gentry (be it for interviewing, or for rights to film on property).

Organisations, Associations and Charities is a self-explanatory area of the site. For the purposes of contributor-finding there are broadly two types of charity or NGO: policy groups, and practitioners (albeit larger organisations will sometimes fall into both camps). When using this section of the site, you do not have to rely on the ability of these organisations to promote themselves on the web, as reflected in web search results – this is a dedicated source. Professional associations (searchable within this section) are also a good way to find specialist contributors. If you want a local historian on Humberside – you may find the professional association (i.e. search local history).

Dictionary of National Biography

The Dictionary of National Biography (www.oxforddnb.com/) is an extensive obituaries database, whose content is generally written and maintained by academics and experts. Although it may be of limited use to time-deprived national news journalists, it can be handy should you venture into features writing, and is especially useful in regional and local journalism. You can approach the site in two ways – searching for an individual by name, or keyword searching the database for places, events, landmarks and movements (or groups). The *People Search* in *Advanced search options* allows you to search by birthplace – an invaluable way for local and regional journalists to establish forgotten local heroes and notables. This source can also help further to develop features. For example, searching for *Clifton suspension bridge* in Free-text will (obviously) not only bring back Isambard Kingdom Brunel's entry, but it will also return other major figures involved in the bridge's construction (such as civil engineer William Henry Barlow), as well as those influenced by the bridge (such as sculptor Kenneth Armitage).

Grove Dictionaries of art and music

As with the Dictionary of National Biography, Grove Art (www.oxfordartonline.com/) and Grove Music (www.oxfordmusiconline.com/) are both niche sources which can nevertheless be used effectively within regional and local journalism. Use the *Biographies* link (in either database) within *Advanced Search* to find artists and musicians by place of birth.

Example: small town Saturday night ...

When training in regional news rooms up and down the country, I have found that searching the Grove databases for births and deaths by local place name will often generate potentially useful subject matter for developing features. These bespoke databases are more thorough than free alternatives when it comes to biographical detail on obscure artists and musicians.

The Times Digital Archive

The Times Digital Archive (archive.timesonline.co.uk/tol/archive/) is an excellent primary newspaper source providing access to *The Times* archive going back to the late 18th century, in the original format in which it was printed. While sometimes used as a source for making astons in broadcasting, it is more often the source of primary research in its own right; *The Thunderer* was, for much of the 19th and 20th centuries, the official organ of state. Several other UK newspaper archives are also available online, including the *Guardian* and *Observer* (http://archive.guardian.co.uk), the *Financial Times* (http://gale.cengage.co.uk/financial-times-historical-archive.aspx), *The Economist* (http://gale.cengage.co.uk/the-economist-historical-archive-18432003.aspx), and collections of *The Daily Mirror*, *The Daily and Sunday Express* and *The Daily Star* (http://www.ukpressonline.co.uk/ukpressonline/open/index.jsp). There are also 19th century newspaper archives (http://www.mediauk.com/article/32686/

newspaper-archives-to-be-found-online). All are necessary in deep, historical journalistic research, because Nexis, Factiva and other archives mainly
deal in post-1990s content. But they can also be really useful for inspiring
a return to a feature topic, or to inspire a topic in a new context.

Encyclopaedia Britannica

It is always worthwhile cross-referencing the factual information you
find with Encyclopaedia Britannica (http://www.britannica.co.uk/).
This is the standard, industry recognised reference tool of choice, albeit
research has shown that it contains equivalent numbers of serious errors
as some of its free counterparts (Giles, 2005).

Events and anniversaries

Significant anniversaries and events (whether past, present or future) are
core to a good deal of features, soft-news and news-diary copy. Thinking
ahead towards forthcoming events (such as the release of government
reports or votes on certain issues), allows journalists to plan in advance
their angle, background and copy. Most media organisations have
subscriptions to databases which help, including:

Entertainment News: (http://www.entnews.co.uk/)
Foresight News (http://www.foresightnews.co.uk/)
Year Ahead (http://www.yearahead.co.uk/)

Some of the larger media groups have databases put together in-house,
but there are plenty of free alternatives on the web.
    A great deal of factual and current affairs programming today is
generated around the anniversaries of significant historical events
(usually in factors of ten years, but sometimes in factors of five). Some
editors find these so-called *handles* editorially lazy and even desperate,
but it is nevertheless possible to derive some value out of historical
facts when woven into the narrative of a story. While isolated historical
facts are not in themselves worthy of news or features coverage, their
significance (such as in the form of a chronology of events) could most
certainly be valid:

BBC On This Day (http://news.bbc.co.uk/onthisday/)

The Wikipedia home page also features an 'on this day' section, but their advanced search options (http://en.wikipedia.org/wiki/Wikipedia:Searching) allow for more thorough searching of past events. Here follow some speculative searches, all of which are angling at a 100-year anniversary of one kind or another (for birth years of famous composers, authors and English poets, respectively):

1910 intitle:composer
1910 -list intitle:author
1910 incategory:English_poets

Those who spend more time looking ahead (as opposed to looking to history) might instead want to use Whats On When, a database used to sell tickets for events, but which contains lots of useful local, regional, national and international event information:

What's on When (http://www.whatsonwhen.com/)

There are other tools for helping to source national and international events including events (elections, publication of reports etc.), such as:

Eventful (http://eventful.com/)
FT Week Ahead (http://www.ft.com/world/weekahead)

Some fairly obvious places to find out what's coming up the arts would include Time Out (http://www.timeout.com), and IMDb Upcoming Releases (http://www.imdb.com/calendar/?region=gb). There are many subject-specific options in hardcopy too (Prospect magazine, for example, has a monthly calendar of talks and other events which is essential forward planning for anyone who takes their philosophy/politics seriously).

Finding PR copy

This is for some most contentious areas of sourcing news, while for others it is an essential part of any journalists' daily routine. There are many online agencies more than willing to distribute tsunamis of copy (and case studies) from those organisations who crave exposure. Here are just a few. Subscriptions, in some cases, may apply – and most of these services require sign-up:

FeaturesExec (http://www.featuresexec.com/)
Gorkana Media Database (http://www.gorkanadatabase.com/)
Pressbox (http://www.pressbox.co.uk/)
Prfire (http://www.prfire.co.uk/)
PR Web (http://ukservice.prweb.com/)
Response Source (http://www.responsesource.com/)
SourceWire (http://www.sourcewire.com/) (Tech and business)

General reference

Wikipedia (http://en.wikipedia.org/wiki/Main_Page) is the leading light in reference material online – but it does not come without its problems, not least the potential to mislead. If you are looking for authoritative, reliable reference website content, then using an open directory, such as DMOZ (http://www.dmoz.org/) or Yahoo Directory (http://dir.yahoo.com/) can be a more effective means of research. Such public directories, put together by dedicated human beings rather than ethereal algorithms, allow you to either browse down or search through. This can be very useful where searching for establishment sources, while trying to avoid the many hoaxes which exist in hyperspace (which are dealt with later in this book).

Henninger (2008) outlines four reasons why researchers should opt for these bespoke, hand-crafted public directories, namely:

Manual classification generally assures the relevancy of the documents within the subject category.

The initial focusing of the search process has been done for you.

By browsing in a broad subject area you should arrive at a more specific aspect of the subject automatically.

Documents on similar subjects are grouped together so all items are potentially relevant.

(Henninger, 2008, p. 61)

However, one major disadvantage of using these tools is the vast difference in volume between automated indexes and manually managed ones. For many searches, directories will simply not have the capacity of content to cope. Further problems with reliance upon open directory content have been explored in the literature. Sherman and Price cite unseen (and so unknown) editorial policies, timeliness, 'lopsided coverage' and the fact that some directories charge website owners for inclusion as mitigating factors (Sherman and Price, 2001, pp. 24–26).

General research aside, there are some sections within the open directory which are especially useful to journalists, not least the following writing aides:

Dictionaries of slang: http://www.dmoz.org/Reference/Dictionaries /World_Languages/E/English/Slang/

Etymological dictionaries: http://www.dmoz.org/Reference /Dictionaries/Etymology/

Homonyms: http://www.dmoz.org/Kids_and_Teens/School_Time /English/Grammar/Homonyms/

Literary dictionaries: http://www.dmoz.org/Reference/Dictionaries /By_Subject/Humanities/

Rhyming Dictionaries: http://www.dmoz.org/Reference/Dictionaries /Rhyming/

Style guides: http://www.dmoz.org/Arts/Writers_Resources /Style_Guides/Grammar/

Thesauri: http://www.dmoz.org/Reference/Thesauri/

Some other useful language tools not connected to the Open Data Project include:

Graphical dictionary: http://www.visuwords.com/

Reverse dictionary: http://onelook.com/reverse-dictionary.shtml

There are many other reference tools on the Web which can be helpful in journalistic research, including search engines, portals, vortals and gateway services. Here follows just a handful of the most useful, from a UK perspective:

InfoPlease (http://www.infoplease.com/): an extensive, world-wide Almanac – features an 'on this day' section for anniversaries.

Intute (http://www.intute.ac.uk/): the largest single collection of academic subject guides and resources, maintained by UK universities.

Nation Master (http://www.nationmaster.com/index.php): useful visual tool containing key economic, political and social indicators from the CIA World Factbook, OECD, World Bank etc.

UK National Statistics' Publication Hub (http://www.statistics.gov.uk/hub/index.html): self-explanatory collection of official UK data.

Wolfram Alpha (http://www.wolframalpha.com/): semantic search engine whose index is comprised of a selection of key data sets, whose purpose geared towards solving scientific and factual problems, and queries.

The World Factbook (https://www.cia.gov/library/publications/the-world-factbook/): the CIA's best annual attempt to publicly analyse countries from around the world.

If you need to contact fellow journalists at other media organisations, ABYZ News (http://www.abyznewslinks.com/) and PaperBoy (http://www.thepaperboy.com/) both offer extensive lists of news media online, and act as free alternative to Willings Press Guide (which is available via some local libraries online collections, in KnowUK).

References

Economist (2009) The decline of the landline, Unwired, August 13: http://www.economist.com/node/14213965

Giles, Jim (2005) Special Report Internet encyclopaedias go head to head, Nature, 438, 900–901 December 15: http://www.nature.com/nature/journal/v438/n7070/full/438900a.html

Henninger, Maureen (2008) *The Hidden Web: Finding Quality Information on the Net (2nd Edition)*. UNSW Press: Sidney.

Long, Johnny (2005) *Google Hacking for Penetration Testers*. Rockland, MA: Syngress Publishing, Inc.

Ryan, Kevin (2008) Must We Unlock the Deep Web?, Search Engine Watch, November 12: http://searchenginewatch.com/3631665

Sherman, Chris and Price, Gary (2001) *The Invisible Web: Uncovering Information Sources Search Engines Can't See*. Information Today, Inc: New Jersey.

University of California, Berkeley (2010) Invisible or Deep Web: What it is, How to find it, and Its inherent ambiguity, UC Berkeley – Teaching Library Internet Workshops, January 08: http://www.lib.berkeley.edu/TeachingLib/Guides/Internet/InvisibleWeb.html

Weaver, David and Bimber, Bruce (2008) 'Finding News Stories: A Comparison of Searches Using Lexis Nexis and Google', *Journalism and Mass Communication Quarterly*, 85(3), 515–530.

Wright, Alex (2009) 'Exploring a 'Deep Web' That Google Can't Grasp, New York Times, February 22: http://www.nytimes.com/2009/02/23/technology/internet/23search.html?th&emc=th

4 Social media theory

>...under the right circumstances, groups are remarkably intelligent and are often smarter than the smartest people in them. Groups do not need to be dominated by exceptionally intelligent people in order to be smart. Even if most of the people within a group are not especially well-informed or rational, it can still reach a collectively wise decision.
>
> (Surowiecki, 2004: p. xiii)

Most journalists are generalists, and as such rely upon the opinions of experts and sources in a range of ways, from only trusting 'news' when they see it published by news agencies, to forming close (Tuchman, 1973), some suggest too close, friendships with politicians, public relations professionals, industry leaders and NGO activists.

These working practices often take place in an environment of private information, which has served journalists well over the years, for good or ill. But in today's many-to-many communications platforms, these cosy, private relationships are coming unstuck. It is now possible for people who have hands-on experience or specialist knowledge concerning news events to broadcast their own 'news', on their own medium, dis-intermediating news media from the story, and so wrecking the exclusivity which drove newspaper journalism. It is now possible for experts and opinion formers to establish themselves as publishers or broadcasters of their own news, and so connect directly to the public. Just as the advent of the electric telegraph helped to establish news as being synonymous with newspapers, so internet technologies now threaten to unpick this semantic connection.

But it would be misleading to think of journalists as perpetual victims of this new state of possibilities. On the contrary, journalists may take advantage of this new publishing landscape, to source actuality and expertise from the great sway of readers (and indeed non-readers) on news stories of the day – and many news media are now deeply engaged in involving their readership in uncovering stories. *The Guardian's* appeals for their readers' help during the MPs' expenses (Rogers, 2009) and Trafigura (Leigh, 2009) scandals, and their Open Newslists (http://www.guardian.co.uk/news/series/open-newslist) experiment are leading lights in a wider industry trend. While newspapers have often made appeals for help in the past, it is now possible for the public to get involved in a very visible and direct way, and for readers to engage in making news in real-time.

This reality has inspired fear in some for the future of journalism, for if journalists lose their status as gatekeepers, as breakers and makers of 'news', then (some feel) they lose their sense of purpose. But these social online tools offer journalists a means of sourcing opinion, expertise and even first-hand evidence about news events from a far wider range of sources than was ever possible before. And while most journalists may be generalists, this does not mean that journalistic skills, insight and ethics are not still crucial to the developing news ecology. Indeed, the importance of these skills today, and for the future, has been expressed convincingly by several authors, conceptualising the rise of Networked Journalism (Beckett, 2008), Grassroots Journalism (Gillmor, 2004), and the shift in journalism from gatekeeping to gatewatching (Bruns, 2005).

In short, journalists need to think of ways to apply their skills and knowledge to events as they break in this online environment. This requires, it is argued, a shift in the focus of journalistic convention – where transparency and openness will become every bit as important as fact-checking, and ethical discretion.

Social networking in the network society

Years before the rise of online social networks, sociologist Manuel Castells had argued that we live in a new epoch, a new technological paradigm where economies are primarily organised around the production and management of information, rather than organised around the production of energy, as they had been throughout the 20th century. It is not that information and knowledge are uniquely crucial in the current age (they arguably always have been in human societies), it is that our new technologies affect our economies, and so our societies, in a more significant way than past information technologies have affected bygone eras. Castells' thesis is predicated on three interwoven elements. The present age, he contends, is informational, global and networked.

The rise of the network is central to this new paradigm. Where once political power was embodied in hierarchical organisations and institutions, it is argued, today that power is spread across networks. Some nodes may be more important to the network than others, but all are essential to the project. Networks are democratic after a fashion; they decentralise power and decision making; they convert power relations into a basic logic of inclusion or exclusion. This is a contentious issue so far as public engagement in journalism is concerned. Online social networks are a self-selecting means of newsgathering – they do not fairly reflect wider society – only one in 20 over 65s engage with social media regularly, and less than one-third of 35–44-year-olds are active online (Ofcom, 2010). Journalists should be careful about how they develop their networks online as exclusivity within an online network does not serve a genuinely pluralist press.

While social networking is not new, its electronic manifestations today is often criticised, even ridiculed, in the mainstream media because the output created is considered to be trivial, (Heffer, 2010) or because the process is considered to be an elitist fad (Street-Porter, 2009). However, these criticisms misunderstand fundamentally that social networks are not a cultural medium, as much as a platform. They are neither an alternative to journalism, nor are they in and of themselves journalism. Twitter, Facebook and other online social tools are a communicative platform, not an end product. They are social media, with the emphasis on social (and all that it connotes). To compare Twitter or Facebook to the conventional media in terms of quality or standards is to misunderstand the essential difference between the two.

Social networking harnesses a many-to-many communicative model, as opposed to the conventional one-to-many model upon which mainstream media was based. As such, it opens the door to anyone with internet access, living outwith oppressive regimes, to join in a global conversation or broadcast their thoughts or experiences to the world. And while we must tread cautiously within such a medium, there are nevertheless opportunities for journalists to get involved in this conversation, and help eke out stories which might otherwise have been ignored.

Newspaper groups make great use of Facebook and other social networks in the distribution of their stories (Jaffe, 2010), but their use in newsgathering and contributor finding is equally significant. Social networks have been a staple source for US journalists for some time (Cison survey, 2010) and they are an increasingly popular source in UK online newsrooms too – research has shown that political reporting has changed irrevocably because of Facebook and Twitter (Newman, 2010).

Facebook even provides a guide to using the platform in journalism: https://www.facebook.com/journalists?sk=app_201416986567309

Being culturally and socially relative, social media have different functions and different groups of users, and this is changing all the time. Today much of Europe, North Africa, North America and India spend time on Facebook, but outliers persist; Poland's fascination with Nasza-klase (http://nk.pl/), Russia's fixation with Kontakte (http://vkontakte.ru/), Brazil's obsession with Orkut (http://www.orkut.com/) and China's love affair with QQ (http://www.qq.com/) remain outwith international trends. There remain many communities wedded to using a social network of choice – and it serves any journalist well to understand who they will likely encounter when seeking out stories, tip-offs and contributors via social networks.

Social networking and online newsgathering – a new ethical space?

As far back as the mid-1970s, the consequences of applying computer technology to medical procedures compelled some, chief among them Walter Maner, to argue that computers were opening up a new ethical space. Some question whether this can be true, arguing that computers do not materially change society, but merely speed up those processes to which they are applied, that we mistake quantitative change for qualitative change. Nonetheless, advances in technology do have consequences for media regulation, and not just with regard to broadcasting bandwidth. The UK Press Complaints Commissions' (PCC) Editor's Code of Practice acknowledged the potential in new technologies to blur the old certainties of public and private space, when in 1993 the definition of private property was tightened, with regard to commercially available advanced long-lens photography. Nevertheless, there are dangers inherent to altering legislation (and regulation) in order to accommodate (and deal with) problems arising out of technological innovation. Whichever philosophical school of thought you use to justify action or agency, it is important to recognise that online scenarios throw up some ethical issues which have no direct equivalent in the physical world.

Respect for online public space

Privacy is an area of ethical concern for developers and users of online services which depend on real-world social structures for their meaning;

this is as true of the personalisation of search, as it is of the rise of social networks. But social networks are also virtual spaces, which can be used to harness a range of different types of relationship. While some argue that privacy is the enemy of free speech, others can point to the European Convention on Human Rights for evidence that privacy is important in Western societies.

Social networks can be private or public spaces, or a hybrid of both. The purpose of an online space is essential in determining how open it is to outside intrusion. For example, commercial networking sites, which exist to help in self-promotion for employment opportunities, are more obviously a public-facing domain than are re-uniting sites, which exist to re-connect individuals who have lost touch with each other, and who want to re-establish personal friendships. Another factor is the nature of site membership. Social networks used predominantly by real-world friends to keep in touch, can be considered to be a more private environment than subject-specific groups, which are open to anyone from anywhere. Use and uptake conventions are also important factors; privacy measures in Facebook are more nuanced than those associated with Twitter (which essentially has a binary privacy status). So for those users who understand these privacy measures (and not all Facebook users do – which is a separate ethical issue) the locus of any user's privacy on Facebook can be plotted on a spectrum, where Twitter users either have private or public accounts. Journalists must take an informed, reasoned and case-specific path through online space, where (ethical matters aside) the risk to reputation for transgression can be significant.

At the more extreme end of privacy intrusion, 'ambulance chasing' is a phenomenon which long pre-dates the advent of the internet, and which has long inspired public opprobrium. Reporters who rushed onto Facebook in order to seek out students caught up in the Virginia Tech shooting atrocity of April 2007, badgered victims and witnesses alike with legitimate accounts, created fake accounts to badger them further, and even created memorials in order to ensnare grieving students. This led many to question the fundamental ethics of journalism in the age of the social network (Hermida, 2007).

In the UK two years later, two *Sunday Express* journalist invaded the privacy of survivors of the Dunblane shooting atrocity who, now teenagers, were found to be doing what most teenagers do on social networks (namely posting details and images of drinking, and swearing). The resulting controversy led to an uncharacteristically robust rebuke from the Press Complaints Commission (PCC, 2009, I) for the *Express*.

The platform which was so egregiously invaded by these *Express* journalists, Bebo (http://www.bebo.com/), is the UK's fourth most popular social network after Facebook, Youtube and Twitter as of June 2010 (Goad, 2010). It is an online community that all journalists should tread very warily around. Almost half of the users on this network are under 17, and the average age of its users is 28 (Royal Pingdom, 2010), significantly younger than other social networks. Given the special consideration journalists must take around minors, it is wise to weigh intrusion into such networks against the very strongest of public interest defences; for most issues it is hard to conceive of a justification, beyond the most traumatic areas of investigative journalism.

Using material found on social networks

The terms 'social media', 'search' and 'Internet' do not feature in the National Union of Journalists Code of Conduct (http://media.gn.apc.org/nujcode.html), or in the PCC Editorial Code of Practice (http://www.pcc.org.uk/cop/practice.html). Indeed, in 2008, following public disquiet about the exploitation of social network information, Tim Toulmin, then Director of the PCC, insisted that guidance on journalist's re-use of social network material need not be written expressly into the PCC code, as it is catered for already (Luft, 2008).

The BBC, which is regulated in a far more intrusive way than the UK press (at the time of writing), suggests this, in its editorial guide:

> Although material, especially pictures and videos, on third party social media and other websites where the public have ready access may be considered to have been placed in the public domain, re-use by the BBC will usually bring it to a much wider audience. We should consider the impact of our re-use, particularly when in connection with tragic or distressing event. (BBC, 2010, II)

Some have argued further that there is even a private sanctuary in public social network accounts; that some users of these services assume a certain amount of privacy due to a 'needle in a haystack' principle which governs how likely information shared is to end up being seen by significant numbers of people (Zimmer, 2010). On the other hand, it may be argued that this approach makes a mockery of the distinction between public and private space. Indeed, a number of cases brought before the PCC, including a policeman who made flippant remarks on his private Facebook account after the unlawful killing of Ian Tomlinson (PCC, 2009, II), and a civil servant who complained about the republication of her tweets (PCC, 2011), have been rejected outright. There is no uniform position on this theme across all UK media, which points to a collective failing in these regulatory regimes.

Using subterfuge online to source news

The PCC has previously ruled that the use of a bogus online identity represents merely 'mild subterfuge', and so is legitimate in the presence of a public interest test (PCC, 2010) (though disclosure in and of itself is construed as a public interest defence, according to the PCC's Editorial Code). So far as the police are concerned, this form of entrapment is considered legitimate at the highest levels, albeit with caveats (Evans and Lewis, 2011). But while such behaviour may be legitimised in regulatory and even legal domains, as an ethical issue, there is a wider debate to be had. Where journalists undertake to use false personas to access closed, private online groups, without disclosing who they are or what their interests are, then they risk straying into deeply unethical territory. This can only fairly be mitigated by a public interest defence with the emphasis on 'important' information, whose impact on society is significant (and not transitory) (Friend and Singer, 2007, p. 81).

This is acknowledged within some media organisations' ethical guidance, including those rules employed at Reuters, which state:

> Reporters must never misrepresent themselves, including in chat rooms and other online discussion forums. They do not 'pick locks' in pursuit of information, nor do they otherwise obtain information illegally. Discovering information publicly available on the web is fair game. Defeating passwords or other security methods is going too far. (Reuters, 2010)

Jeff Jarvis (2008) has argued that source transparency is replacing objectivity (or 'balance') as a new guiding ethic in journalism online – this notion is predicated upon the central, functional importance of the hyperlink in online communications as the glue which holds the Web together. Others maintain that such technologically determinist notions should not simply be allowed to trample over basic, universal human needs (such as privacy). Elsewhere, and more subtly, it is argued that attitudes to privacy are being challenged by the new ways people share information about themselves, and re-construct their lives online (Solove, 2008).

Some question the legitimacy of the 'off the record' principle on entirely separate grounds, arguing that journalists have every right to employ subterfuge in terms of identity (Niles, 2008), because there is a deeper problem with the struggle between transparency and privacy online. Such perspectives factor without the sanctity of personal privacy (whether on the part of the journalist, sources or members of the public). The psychological importance for journalist and public alike to be able to communicate without fear or favour, to reason through complicated issues, to voice the unthinkable 'offline', where otherwise the consequences of sharing such information would be massively damaging to careers, cannot be ignored. While the primacy of the First Amendment informs some US thinkers, in the UK human rights legislation and conventions (and media regulations which pre-date them) recognise the importance and sanctity of personal privacy (in principle at least).

Some media organisations have sought to obviate the issue of 'objectivity' in their reporting by laying down rules and regulations about how staff conduct themselves in public (and private) capacities online. The BBC's social media guidelines can be seen to be merging professional and public space online, certainly as far as editorial journalists are concerned:

> Editorial staff and staff in politically sensitive areas should never indicate a political allegiance on social networking sites, either through profile information or through joining political groups. This is particularly important for all staff in News and Current Affairs, Nations and Regions and factual programming and applies regardless of whether they indicate that they are employed by the BBC or not. (BBC, 2010, I)

In 2009 the *Washington Post's* social media guidelines were leaked, showing that some media companies were going a step further than the BBC. The document encouraged *Post* journalists to engage with political individuals, groups and movements online, but to be seen to be doing so in a 'balanced' way:

> Our online data trails reflect on our professional reputations and those of The Washington Post. Be sure that your pattern of use does not suggest, for example, that you are interested only in people with one particular view of a topic or issue. (Kramer, 2009)

This attempt at 'keeping up appearances' represents for some an absurd last ditch, shoring up a convention whose time has (at long last) passed. The principle of 'objectivity' in news (which has its critics), owes its origins not just to the potential in new technologies from the late 19th century, but also to the advertisers who, demanding access to mass-market audiences, provided the cash-flow which kept print news in business from the mid-19th century onwards (at least according to a classical liberal reading of the history of the press). While some may question the significance of who we follow, or in what we re-publish online in terms of our own views, networked space clearly has serious implications for the scrutiny of 'objectivity' in news, and for news publishers and journalists.

Rupert Murdoch says sorry: legally and illegally sourced news

On Saturday July 16, 2011, the UK's national newspapers all ran with an extraordinary advertisement, an unavoidably humiliating apology from the most powerful and influential news baron on the planet: Rupert Murdoch. Published the day after Murdoch lost two of his most senior executives in Les Hinton and Rebekah Brooks, this was a long-overdue apology for the long-denied illegal news-gathering techniques employed by his journalists at *The News of the World*. Aside from bugging the phones of celebrities and senior politicians, journalists at this top-selling Sunday newspaper had hacked the phones of murder victims, victims of terrorist atrocities, and even those soldiers killed on duty whose rights the newspaper sought to campaign on behalf of.

Thirteen days before, the final edition of *The News of the World* rolled off the Waping presses. That day's copy bore contrasting emotions. On the one hand, there was contrition for the illegality that had led to the newspapers' demise, but on the other hand, a familiar self-congratulatory braggadocio concerning the papers' 'proud' record of journalism. Shameless and conflicted to the end, The News of the World died because their brand of storming, salacious, scandalous journalism relied too heavily on illegal methods of obtaining information.

But *The News of the World* was not alone in sourcing illicitly obtained information from private investigators in this way; on the contrary, a report by the Information Commissioner in 2006, *What Price Our Privacy*, showed that such practice was widespread throughout the UK news media. Operation Motorman traced illicitly obtained information which included 'details of criminal records, registered keepers of vehicles, driving licence details, ex-directory telephone numbers, itemised telephone billing and mobile phone records, and details of "Friends & Family" telephone numbers' (Information Commissioner's Office, 2006) to 305 named journalists from across the UK newspaper industry.

For the most part these illegal practices relate to offline news-gathering routines (phone-hacking, illegally obtaining personal information, 'blagging' etc.), and so fall outwith the remit of this book. But it is also alleged that the illicit use of malware (or Trojans; programs sent often via email attachment to infect computers, which then allow the sender to log keystrokes, and monitor use of the computer) also abounded within this arm of Rupert Murdoch's News Corp empire.

While there is today a critical mass of information in the public domain about the scale of phone-hacking at News International, it is as yet uncertain how widespread the exploitation of computer hacking may have been. We have the anecdotal evidence of a former Prime Minister made in parliament (Brewster, 2011), anecdotal evidence from two celebrity bloggers (Leyden, 2011) and a Panorama documentary which proved that emails belonging to a former British Intelligence operative were hacked by a private detective, and obtained by then News of the World editor Alex Marunchak (BBC News, 2011). It remains to be seen just what lessons can be learned here; and two UK parliamentary enquiries (not to mention an FBI enquiry) will likely shed more light over the coming years.

It is the industrialisation of these practices at News International that makes their illegality and immorality all the harder to justify. When such practices become routine (rather than a last resort, when all legal methods have been exhausted), then this threatens to undermine the very public interest defence that investigative journalism has always relied upon to hold the corrupt to account in the UK. In a country whose legal system permits the rich and powerful (both individuals and corporations) to super-injunct legitimate investigation into, and criticism of their behaviour, the phone-hacking scandal may yet pose a serious danger to the proper functioning of British democracy.

But while leading politicians and public figures, and even some journalists (Bould, 2011), have framed these events as a crisis for British journalism, others might contend that this could not be further from the truth. After all, it was the relentless and fearless investigating undertaken by Nick Davies (and others) at *The Guardian* over several years, during which time threats, smears and casual dismissals were thrown at them by those implicated (among them some of the most powerful figures in contemporary British life). Today we can say Rupert Murdoch has experienced his Watergate (Bernstein, 2011), though the consequences for News Corp remain to be seen. Nevertheless, it is a credit to British journalism, in the pursuit of the public interest which drove Davies that we now know what we know; and that we can move on.

References

BBC (2010, I) Editorial Guidelines: Social Networking, Microblogs and other Third Party Websites: Personal Use: http://www.bbc.co.uk/guidelines /editorialguidelines/page/guidance-blogs-personal-full

BBC (2010, II) Editorial Guidelines: Privacy and Consent: http://www.bbc. co.uk/guidelines/editorialguidelines/page/guidelines-privacy-privacy-consent/#material-from-social-media

BBC News (2011) News of the World executive obtained hacked e-mails, BBC News, March 14: http://www.bbc.co.uk/news/uk-12712400

Beckett, Charlie (2008) *SuperMedia – Saving Journalism so it can Save the World.* WileyBlackwell: London.

Bernstein, Carl (2011) Murdoch's Watergate?, Newsweek, July 11: http://www. newsweek.com/2011/07/10/murdoch-s-watergate.html

Bould, Sarah (2011) NoW scandal has 'sullied the name of journalism', Hold The Front Page, July 13: http://www.holdthefrontpage.co.uk/2011/news/scandal-has-sullied-the-name-of-journalism-says-men-editor/

Brewster, Tom (2011) The former Prime Minister says Trojans were used by the now deceased tabloid as the hacking scandal rages on, IT PRO, July 14: http://www. itpro.co.uk/634912/gordon-brown-claims-malware-used-in-notw-hacking

Bruns, Axel (2005) *Gatewatching: Collaborative Online News Production.* Peter Lang Publishing: New York.

Castells, Manuel (2000) 'Material for an exploratory theory of the network society', *British Journal of Sociology*, 51(1), 5–24.

Cison survey (2010) Journalists' use of social media for research increases, but traditional media are still seen as more reliable: http://insight.cision.com /content/GWU-request

Evans, Rob and Lewis, Paul (2011) Met chief says officers' use of fake identities in court was not illegal, The Guardian, October 27: http://www.guardian.co.uk /uk/2011/oct/27/met-police-activists-fake-identities

Friend, Cecelia and Singer, Jane (2007) *Online Journalism Ethics, Traditions and Transitions.* ME Sharpe: New York.

Gillmor, Dan (2006) *We The Media: Grassroots Journalism by the People for the People.* O'Reilly Media, Inc: New York.

Goad, Robin (2010) Social networks now more popular than search engines in the UK, June 08: http://weblogs.hitwise.com/robin-goad/2010/06/social_ networks_overtake_search_engines.html

Heffer, Simon (2009) Facebook: Everything you never wanted to know..., Telegraph, June 13: http://www.telegraph.co.uk/comment/columnists/simonheffer /5524402/Facebook-Everything-you-never-wanted-to-know....html

Hermida, Alfred (2007) Social media poses digital dilemmas for journalists, Journalism Ethics, June 08: http://www.journalismethics.info/feature_arti-cles/social_media_poses_digital_dilemmas.htm

Information Commissioner's Office (2006) What Price Privacy? The unlawful trade in confidential personal information: http://www.ico.gov.uk/upload/documents/library/corporate/research_and_reports/what_price_privacy.pdf

Jaffe, Alexandra (2010) Facebook Social Plugins and Open Graph: What they mean for online newspapers, Editors' Weblog, April 22: http://www.editorsweblog.org/analysis/2010/04/facebook_social_plugins_and_open_graph_w.php

Jarvis, Jeff (2008) On Transparency versus Objectivity, Big Think (video): http://bigthink.com/ideas/1260

Kramer, Staci (2009) WaPo's Social Media Guidelines Paint Staff Into Virtual Corner; Full Text of Guidelines, paid Content, September 27: http://paidcontent.org/article/419-wapos-social-media-guidelines-paint-staff-into-virtual-corner/

Leigh, David (2009) Trafigura drops bid to gag Guardian over MP's question, The Guardian, October 13: http://www.guardian.co.uk/media/2009/oct/13/trafigura-drops-gag-guardian-oil

Leyden, John (2011) 'I caught a virus from Murdoch's organ' – famous secret hooker, Malware de Jour also hit Girl With One-Track Mind, The Register, July 12: http://www.theregister.co.uk/2011/07/12/malware_de_jour/

Luft, Oliver (2008) Social networks need to do more to raise awareness about misuse of personal information, says PCC director, Journalism.co.uk, June 05: http://www.journalism.co.uk/news/social-networks-need-to-do-more-to-raise-awareness-about-misuse-of-personal-information-says-pcc-director/s2/a531706/

Newman, Nic (2010) #UKelection2010, mainstream media and the role of the internet: how social and digital media affected the business of politics and journalism. Reuters Institute for the Study of Journalism: Oxford University, July 6.

Niles, Robert (2008) There's no such thing as 'off the record' anymore, Online Journalism Review, April 16: http://www.ojr.org/ojr/stories/080416niles-on-the-record/

Ofcom (2010) UK Adults' Media Literacy Report, May 17: http://stakeholders.ofcom.org.uk/market-data-research/media-literacy/medlitpub/medlitpubrss/adultmedialitreport/

Press Complains Commission (PCC) (2009, I) Ms Mullan, Mr Weir & Ms Campbell vs Scottish Sunday Express adjudication, June 22: http://www.pcc.org.uk/news/index.html?article=NTc5Mw==?oxid=a8ea2047270292dc8f98ecbcb23a6d0c

Press Complaints Commission (PCC) (2009, II) PCC rejects privacy complaint about Facebook comments, December 02: http://www.pcc.org.uk/news/index.html?article=NjA4Mg==

Press Complaints Commission (PCC) (2010) Mr Paul Smith vs Hull Daily Mail adjudication, July 27: http://www.pcc.org.uk/news/index.html?article=NjU0Mg==

Press Complaints Commission (PCC) (2011) Ms Sarah Baskerville, February 08: http://www.pcc.org.uk/news/index.html?article=NjkzNA==

Reuters (2010) Social Media Guidelines: http://handbook.reuters.com/index.php/Reporting_from_the_internet#Social_media_guidelines

Rogers, Simon (2009) How to crowdsource MPs' expenses, The Guardian, June 18: http://www.guardian.co.uk/news/datablog/2009/jun/18/mps-expenses-houseofcommons

Royal Pingdom (2010) Study: Ages of social network users, Royal Pingdom, February 16: http://royal.pingdom.com/2010/02/16/study-ages-of-social-network-users/

Solove, Daniel J. (2008) Do Social Networks Bring the End of Privacy? *Scientific American Magazine*, September.

Street-Porter, Janet (2009) Editor-At-Large: Twitter ye not, for it will not change the world, August 16: http://www.independent.co.uk/opinion/columnists/janet-street-porter/editoratlarge-twitter-ye-not-for-it-will-not-change-the-world-1772833.html

Surowiecki, James (2005) *The Wisdom of Crowds*. Abacus: London.

Tuchman, G (1973) 'Making news by doing work: Routinizing the unexpected', *American Journal of Sociology*, 79(1), 110–131.

Zimmer, Michael (2010) Is it Ethical to Harvest Public Twitter Accounts without Consent?, MichaelZimmer.org, December 02: http://michaelzimmer.org/2010/02/12/is-it-ethical-to-harvest-public-twitter-accounts-without-consent/

5 Social networks and newsgathering

Introduction

There are many social networks available to journalists who need to make contacts and source news. Here follows a close look at how to use these sources, including an overview of their relative potential as people finders.

Facebook

Since 2009, Facebook (http://www.facebook.com/) users have rapidly been getting older (Schroder, 2009) – those aged between 35 and 54 are joining at a higher rate than all other age groups – though all age groups are (at the time of writing) increasing on Facebook, as reflected in the landmark half-a-billion users milestone achieved in July 2010 (Myslewski, 2010). In the US, research has shown that more affluent, and more urban users will likely be heavier social networkers, and that Facebook users are on average more affluent than, for example, Myspace users (Nielsen Wire, 2009). The average Facebook user is 38 (Royal Pingdom, 2010), but in the UK the greatest number of users is aged between 18 and 25 (Su, 2010). Facebook users are, on average, more female than male (Royal Pingdom, 2009). But these figures have changed significantly over time (Social Media Optimisation, 2008), and will no doubt continue to do so.

It has been argued that in the long-term, Facebook could become a genuine rival to Google in search, as we move towards seeking out information filtered through the interests of our friends and contacts online (Goodman, 2009). In any case, social networks are, as of June 2010, more popular than search in the UK (Goad, 2010). Many of Facebook's users are interested in international, social and political issues, and some are experts in their field – the site contains groups based around themes and issues from around the world.

Facebook requires you to sign up in order to make any meaningful use of it. At first glance it does not seem a difficult site to search, but when results come back, it is worth bearing in mind the various filters which comprise this particular social network (listed as *navigation* on the left- hand side of search results). The *People* option lets you search for people by name – allowing refined results by location, school or work-place (or a combination of these) once your initial results are returned. It is possible to put a place name into people search, but these results can be inconsistent. There will be groups for place names which are more inclusive, but they may contain many people with a connection to the place in question, rather than current residents. On the other hand, those people found by place-name search may have moved else-where without updating their profile, not to mention the many people who have not bothered to populate this field in their profile. You can search for profiles by email address if you have one – this is one of the few mass-market online tools which allow this.

Pages can be useful for padding out a geographical beat. Try search-ing for the place names in your beat and become a fan of these pages to keep up on issues both trivial and serious. There are, at the time of writ-ing, over 500 pages featuring the term 'peterborough' – many (though not all) of them will be relevant to a journalist whose beat includes this town. The same could be said for *Groups* – which differ from Pages insofar as they denote a sense of activity in their members, rather than a loose association, or general interest in something (say a brand, a celebrity or an institution). Groups can be especially useful in tracking future events – membership is controlled and the privacy settings and responsibilities involved can make for a more personal, as opposed to corporate or general network, experience.

If you have developed a healthy following, *Posts by Friends* can be a good place to search for interesting news. *Posts by Everyone* lets you find publicly shared status updates from all of Facebook – be aware though that many people choose not to make their status updates public. Facebook encountered severe criticism when, in 2009, it made all status updates public by default – inspiring some concerned indi-viduals to shame the company into changing its policy by making all of these updates easily searchable in Your Open book (site now defunct). Otherwise, you can browse for contributors by a number of criteria including place and employer (http://www.facebook.com/find-friends/browser/).

Applications: there have been, during Facebook's history, some very useful Facebook applications for journalists, which are now defunct (including Advanced Search 2.2 Beta for general search and Truescoop for finding US citizens with criminal records). One app which continues to prove its worth however is the Facebook Chat History Manager add-on (https://addons.mozilla.org/en-us/firefox/addon/facebook-chat-history-manager/) for Firefox (or Chrome). This tool ensures that your Facebook conversations are stored for later (just in case you delete your inbox).

It has long been rumoured (Van Grove, 2010) that Bing will incorporate public Facebook status updates into its index; however, at the time of writing, Bing's social vertical (http://www.bing.com/social) does not yet appear to provide them. Neither are they available in Google, for now. But that is not to say that conventional search engines can not help you make sense of Facebook content in ways which the site's own search does not allow. Facebook has many public topic pages, forums which bring people together around different issues – but the content of these conversations is not searchable within Facebook. As an example, try the following domain search in Google in conjunction with a search term you are interested in:

site:facebook.com/topic bbc

Because Google indexes the whole web page, keywords buried in text (and not present in topic titles or names) can be found – this can be a hugely useful means of digging out obscure information for the purposes of search, or for reputation management.

Twitter

One of the principle advantages of using Twitter (https://twitter.com/) over Facebook and many other social networks, is that you do not have to have an account to make use of its research and news-gathering potential. Though of course in terms of actually communicating with others and building both your reputation and your online contacts, it certainly helps.

Sixty-four per cent of Twitter users are over 35 (Royal Pingdom, 2010). By November 2009, the UK had 5.5 million 'Tweepz'. According to a YouGov survey in 2009, Twitter users are younger than average, more likely to vote Labour, more liberal, more London-centric (and less Northern) and more likely members of lower social classes (Sparrow,

2009). It is not, however, as popular with users in their teens, according to research undertaken by Morgan Stanley a few months earlier (Kollewe, 2009). The conventions used on Twitter have traditionally been driven by its users, but more recently the group has published a guide to Twitter use in newsrooms (http://media.twitter.com/newsrooms).

Anatomy of a tweet

Though it is not essential to get involved in Twitter in order to find news, it is nevertheless useful to understand some of the basic short-hand conventions of the medium. Here is a simple primer:

A tweet sharing a link to a Radio 4 Documentary, 'Heroes and Hacks' presented by Eamonn O'Neill

MT (Modified Tweet): This tweet, has been edited from the original by the author @Murray_Dick, and so 'MT' is used to signify that changes have been made. The edited tweet has then been re-tweeted (RT) by a third user, and so shared with their followers (you can see this user's avatar below the message, and the programme summary). This can be done manually (by typing out MT or RT before a re-published message), but is automated in some Twitter client platforms.

.**@eamonnoneill**: This is the intended recipient of this tweet (albeit, everyone else is effectively copied in, by means of the full-stop just before the @ sign). Users can send private Tweets (or direct messages) which will not appear publicly too.

#Watergate: The # symbol is used to develop keyword-driven topics, to focus everyone's conversation around a particular theme (in this case the Watergate scandal). It can be quite a messy process finding trending topics, but their distribution is very much bound up in the social nature of the medium. That is to say, someone starts up a trending topic, which their friends can see and contribute to, and which then in turn their friends' friends can contribute to, and so on. If you want to find out if a trending topic for a subject exists, just try out some speculative efforts in the Twitter search box. Trending topics in Twitter are discussed in more detail later in this chapter.

bbc.in/109Y7OL: Given the 140-character limit on tweets, it is important to be able to shorten any link you want to share with one of many url shortening services – something Twitter does automatically. There are alternatives (i.e. bit.ly, or tinyurl.com), and all are worthy information sources in their own right. You can search the bit.ly index for content around a theme, which will show you relevance by social discovery, rather than search engine algorithm.

For those who do not want a Twitter account, there is a separate advanced search (https://twitter.com/#!/search-advanced). Full Boolean options are available, as well as a hashtag search option (for searching out trending topics – prefixed with a #). The *People* filters are fairly limiting, and the *Attitudes* filter extends sentiment analysis only so far as the use of emoticons in posts (which is not particularly helpful for seeking out hard news stories). The *Containing links* option can be used to dig out conversations around links or even multimedia. The full list operators (which can be used in simple search) includes the following:

To find tweets by a user, use from: <username>
To find tweets to a user, use to: <username>
To find a tweet from someone near a place, use near:"aberdeen"
To specify the approximate distance of the tweeter from a place, use
   within:25k (where k = kilometres. Can also use m for miles)

To find tweets posted since a particular date, use since:2012–12–09 (this uses US date format)
To find tweets posted before a particular date use until:2012–12–09
To find tweets containing URLs, use filter:links

The real value in this search tool is in the *Places* option – whether used on its own or in conjunction with other search terms and options. It will return people based either on the location they have typed into their profile (which may or may not be reliable), or if they have enabled the *Tweet with your location* option when using Twitter on a mobile device.

Once you have a keyword search, you may want to create a Really Simple Syndication (RSS) feed for it to help you keep on top of your beat – more detail on RSS can be found later in Chapter 7. This is not a simple process in the current web interface (it is worth remembering that many users access the service via third-party applications and sites). To get an RSS feed by keyword, use the following URL, replacing <keyword> with your own search term:

http://search.twitter.com/search.rss?q=<insert keyword>

For setting up RSS Twitter feeds with more elements, here follow a number of templates which can be altered using your own keywords and other search parameters:

To keep a user's timeline: http://twitter.com/statuses/user_timeline/<insert user ID>.rss
(you will require the user's unique identifying number for this, which can be found via www.idfromuser.com/)
Trending topic feed: http://search.twitter.com/search.atom?q=%<insert topic>
User mention search feed: http://search.twitter.com/search.atom?q=%40<insert username>
Multiple keyword feed: http://search.twitter.com/search.atom?q=<insert keyword 1>+<insert keyword 2>
Either/or keyword feed: http://search.twitter.com/search.atom?q=<insert keyword 1>+OR+<insert keyword 2>
Geo-location keyword feed: http://search.twitter.com/search.atom?geocode=<insert longitude>%2C<insert latitude>%2C<insert radius>mi&q=+<insert keyword 1>+<insert keyword 2>

To find the GPS coordinates for physical locations, run a place search in Google Maps and then copy the *Embed code*, found in the *Share* option. Look through this code for a number directly preceded by an 'equal sign'; this is the longitude for your location, and immediately after this (separated by a comma) is the latitude.

Hacked URL:

http://search.twitter.com/search.atom?geocode=51.501166%2C-0.14227%2C0.2mi

Code:

```
<iframe width="425" height="350" frameborder="0" scrolling="no" marginheight="0"
marginwidth="0" src="http://maps.google.co.uk/maps?
f=q&amp;source=s_q&amp;hl=en&amp;geocode=&amp;q=buckingham+palace&amp;aq=
&amp;sll=51.479902,-
0.565436&amp;sspn=0.006268,0.021136&amp;g=sl39hl&amp;ie=UTF8&amp;hq=bucking
ham+palace&amp;t=h&amp;ll=51.501166,-
0.14227&amp;spn=0.006295,0.006295&amp;output=embed"></iframe><br /><small><a
href="http://maps.google.co.uk/maps?
f=q&amp;source=embed&amp;hl=en&amp;geocode=&amp;q=buckingham+palace&amp;a
q=&amp;sll=51.479902,-
0.565436&amp;sspn=0.006268,0.021136&amp;g=sl39hl&amp;ie=UTF8&amp;hq=bucking
ham+palace&amp;t=h&amp;ll=51.501166,-0.14227&amp;spn=0.006295,0.006295"
style="color:#0000FF;text-align:left">View Larger Map</a></small>
```

Embedding code from Google maps: note GPS coordinates in bold

Be wary of using conventional place names in search – duplicate place names from around the world will cause problems, and US users are still far more prevalent on Twitter than are UK users. Twitter no longer supports geo-spatial coordinate searching, nor post code searching, but you can track down the coordinates of individual Tweepz using the freeware creepy (http://ilektrojohn.github.com/creepy/).

To filter results so that you see only those linking to pictures, videos and other media shared on popular networks, try the following search:

yfrog OR twitpic OR tweetphoto OR snaptweet OR twiddeo OR
    twitvid near:edinburgh within:10k

This will return tweets posted within 10 kilometres of Edinburgh which contain links to some of the more popular media-sharing Twitter services. This can be particularly useful for seeking out images from near a breaking news event, though it will inevitably include irrelevant images if the place in question is a big city. If you find this approach returns results from other Edinburghs, try searching in Trendsmap (http://trendsmap.com/), which disambiguates place names by country.

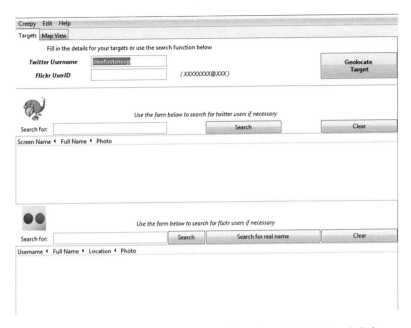

Cree.py's interface: this tool was developed by Infosecurity enthusiast Yiannis Kakavas

Searching older tweets is a serious problem in Twitter – Twitter's own web-based search results can go back several years but are nevertheless very selective (Burstein, 2013). US searchers may be able to access Twitter's archives via an Updates option in search results (which draws selectively from the Library of Congress archive of all tweets). As of late 2009, many tweets have been indexed on Google (Bunz, 2009). so Google's domain function (covered earlier in this book) can be instructive here. Try the following search:

budget site: *http://twitter.com/*/status*

This should find archived tweets mentioning the budget from any user (note the use of the wildcard for the folder preceding */status*).

Those who syndicate their tweets via FriendFeed have a far deeper searchable archive. However, it is worth bearing in mind that even those services with access to the Twitter 'firehose' (direct API) do not have anything even approaching a complete Twitter archive, so it is important to try different services. In the absence of the now-defunct Google Realtime search, which took advantage of the 'firehose', the most comprehensive archive of tweets can be accessed via Topsy (http://topsy.com/). Some other tools which are useful for searching Twitter's archive include:

Searchtastic (http://www.searchtastic.com/)
The Archivist (archive your own and selected tweets) (http://archivist.visitmix.com)
Tweetboard (Alpha invite at time of writing) (http://tweetboard.com/alpha/)
Tweetscan (backup option may help) (https://www.tweetscan.com/index.php)

The problem of archiving in Twitter may be allayed more permanently (and thoroughly) once the Library of Congress, who have acquired all Twitter data, make it publicly available (albeit some archive material is available to access for businesses, via marketing company Datasift). There are more tools for digging out archived tweets which can be found later in this chapter, in the section *Real-time search*.

Twitter works especially well as a news-gathering source when you have a large pool of people to follow, and in turn, a large number of followers whose tweets can inform your newsgathering. But how do you acquire a large and meaningful following? At a very basic level, you can go through the process of finding all your email contacts on sign up to Twitter. You can also perform a basic search for names you know, then once you have found them, go through their followers (and their Twitter lists) to see who else may be worth following. Browsing through hashtags, trending topics, individual posts (and their associated profiles and lists) is a good (if laborious) way to dig out potential contributors around certain topics. But there are a number of dedicated directories which are worth bearing in mind when it comes to expertise or experience.

Follower Wonk (http://followerwonk.com/) provides a search for Twitter profiles, which can be essential if you are searching for people by profession, location or interests, and especially a combination of these. The results show you how many updates each person has made – which can show you how proactive a user they are, which in turn may suggest not only how well connected they are in their field online, but also how likely they will be to get back to you within a short deadline, via Twitter.

Users of Twitter might assume that URL-shortening tools are all about distributing content, but they can have a research and contributor-finding value too. The leading URL-shortening service bit.ly (https://bitly.com/) provides analysis which lets you track the flow of your links shared via the service, not to mention clicks on those links over time (see the Manage tab – login to Twitter account required). Searching for URLs using Twitter Advanced search is not reliable, and would not include shortened links. But it can be a useful way to find people motivated by certain issues. This can in turn feed into developing your own Twitter following and your own pool of contacts.

Conversations between individual accounts can be hard to track on Twitter, but can be the source of intriguing information; Aaron Swartz has created a tool which can help with this (http://twitter.theinfo.org/). You can obtain a tweet's individual ID by clicking on its time stamp. There are many other Twitter-related research tools, which will be introduced later in this chapter. For help on using Twitter, take a look at their Help Center (http://support.twitter.com/) and Get Satisfaction (http://getsatisfaction.com/twitter) forums.

Other social networks

Google+ (https://plus.google.com/): with more than 90 million users as of January 2012 (Wasserman, 2012), this platform has been feted as a long-term challenger to both Facebook and Twitter. This platform offers real potential in newsgathering, not least from the 'hang out' option, a mass-video conferencing facility, which can be used to group-chat with news sources. When launched, its terms of service insisted upon real-name disclosure, a policy which may serve the purposes of transparent, objective news coverage, but which militates against whistleblowing. It has been stated though that this policy is due for overhaul (Galperin and York, 2011). At the time of writing, there is a major US bias in users and in content and a lack of any real activity around anything other than the most popular UK news topics. Another late arrival to social networking, Pinterest (http://pinterest.com/) is a life-streaming platform which boasts a significant, and overwhelmingly, female userbase (Constine, 2012). Again however, it lacks a UK focus at the time of writing.

FriendFeed (http://friendfeed.com/) has far fewer users than Twitter (and indeed some Twitter users duplicate their feeds via FriendFeed, and visa versa). Its advanced search (http://friendfeed.com/search/advanced) offers a range of options to keep up on issues. Tumblr search (http://www.tumblr.com/search) can be inconsistent, and there is no formalised profile element to search within in this platform.

Myspace (http://www.myspace.com/), UK's fifth most popular social network, has a significant under-17-year-old userbase – 33% according to the latest research (Royal Pingdom, 2010). That said, many older people use Myspace too. Myspace does not have an advanced search, but it does offer various means of filtering your search results, whether by channel (people, music, videos and images) or by demographic factors (such as gender, or age). Myspace offers groups, and, as with Facebook, it has public forums which can be searched in Google using the domain function:

london site:forums.myspace.com

Hi5 (http://hi5.com/) and Netlog (http://en.netlog.com/) have significant UK users, though far fewer than Facebook and Twitter.

If you are looking for professional communities then, aside from Facebook's networks, LinkedIn (http://uk.linkedin.com/) is probably the best resource. LinkedIn is a social networking site aimed at the professional community – for those seeking contacts and jobs in their industries. Although there's a heavy US presence here, LinkedIn contains a sizeable range of UK-based professionals. Registration is not necessary to search, albeit it will allow you to make contact and seek out introductions to people. If you want to send mails, request more than five introductions at a time or see expanded results, you will need to buy a Pro account (there are different levels of access, at different tariffs). LinkedIn can be especially useful for seeking out people by employer – present or past. This can be a good means of approaching a sensitive issue, or an issue where employees are being discouraged from talking to the press.

Example: follow the money (even when it has disappeared)...

While training in a London newsroom on the day Lehman Brothers filed for bankruptcy, I was told that journalists prowling the bars around Canary Wharf were having little success in sourcing information (due to the legal agreements employees had signed). But a search of LinkedIn highlighted the names of those who used to work at the stricken investment bank, which proved to be an alternative, indirect means of accessing opinion and experience of events.

LinkedIn is best used when a work-related research problem arises – people will not necessarily treat their LinkedIn account in the same social way as they would with a Facebook account – they may be well established in their field and do not need to share this information with the wider world. As an alternative to LinkedIn, there is Xing (http://www.xing.com/). The average user on this network is aged 44 (Royal Pingdom, 2010).

If you need to find older contributors, Sagazone (http://www.saga-zone.co.uk/) is a good alternative. Likewise, if you are looking for people according to the school they once attended, Friends Reunited (http://www.friendsreunited.com/) and My Old Mate (http://www.myoldmate.net/) often offer a more nuanced means of finding people than do Facebook's school pages.

Perhaps the best place to start looking for specialist groups online is among those services which allow online communities to create their own social networks. Try searching Ning (http://www.ning.com/) or SocialGo (http://www.socialgo.com). Google Profiles search (http://www.google.com/profiles) should not be discounted; they may not include contact details, but can give an insight into potential contributors.

If you have set up accounts for some of these sources, you may want to be able to follow them all from one source. There are a few services which can help here such as CollectedIn (http://collectedin.com/) and AOL Lifestream (http://lifestream.aol.com/), both of which allow you to log in to each of your accounts, and keep on top of them all from the same page.

Mobile social networks

The rise of the smart phone has made possible some very intuitive and innovative ways to find people and engage with communities. Mobile social networks are often considered in terms of game-play; where users are rewarded for performing a task (something which lends itself well to commercial and PR professionals). But in marrying social networking and geo location, mobile social networks can provide an alternative means of finding sources; establishing impromptu meetings or even tracking the development of a story as it is unfolding in real time, geographically.

UK data journalist Nicola Hughes has offered insight into the innovative use of the geolocation function available via these social media platforms. When using Foursquare in conjunction with Google Maps, Nicola was able to find, and then verify, the reliability of a potential witness to a volcanic eruption in Indonesia, despite the scale of 'background noise' created in trending topics from this region at the time (Hughes, 2011).

There are several options out there; the most popular being:

BrightKite (http://brightkite.com/)
Foursquare (https://foursquare.com/)
Gowalla (http://gowalla.com/)
Plazes (http://plazes.com/)

Online forums

Google's *Discussions* vertical contains Google Groups (https://groups. google.com/?hl=en), which in turn incorporates Usenet newsgroups dating back to 1981. This is arguably the most comprehensive forum to seek out contributors and to keep up to date on your beat or topic area on the web. A good way into Google Groups is to search for general, topical keywords within the 'search for a group' search bar. The menu of results allows you to filter by region, topic, post frequency, volume of members, language (which differentiates between US and UK English) and the number of days since last post. The last filter is perhaps the most useful in news and current affairs contributor-finding and news-gathering, as those groups which have had little activity over the past month may be less likely to yield a response to short deadlines. Groups can be generalist or specialist, serious or trivial – there are many groups comprised exclusively of academics, professionals and experts of all kinds, and indeed some of the most popular groups require (free) membership.

Given the depth of archive, it is always a good idea to sort results by date rather than relevance – people may have given up their accounts in the ten years since they posted the messages you have just found. The advanced search in Google Groups (http://groups.google.com/ advanced_search?q=&safe=on&) provides one of the few means of online search by email domain. A search for @bbc.co.uk, for example, returns many messages posted by BBC journalists and researchers seeking out contributors. Be wary though – newsgroups are closed communities, often organised around issues and hobbies taken seriously. It is unwise to barge into online forums assuming everyone there will be awed by your profession, and assuming they will respond in kind. Treat newsgroup contributors with tact and civility – do not belittle hobbies, or come across as taking but not giving back, if you want to make the most of these forums.

Yahoo Groups (http://groups.yahoo.com/) is a worthy alternative, with conversational content reaching back to 1988. This is a less utilitarian tool for day-to-day work – their advanced search (http://groups.yahoo.com/group/flyfishermensretreat/msearch_adv) is limiting. Whether public or private, access to these groups often requires sign up, but some of the bigger groups are updated very frequently – it's a good idea to include a location in your searching to avoid the US bias in membership.

Omgili (http://omgili.com/) is a crawler-based service which can be thought of as a metasearch engine for forums dotted around the web – use this tool to find general chatter across forums, discussion groups and mailing lists. It can be a great source of unofficial information, but given the often-anonymous nature of forums, it is not the most reliable of sources. There is an advanced search option on results pages, but the sliding-scale options for time scale, number of replies and number of commenters, give more than enough scope to filter out passing references and irrelevant pages. At the time of writing, they offer two RSS options; a (paid) premium option which provides near real-time content, sorted by date, and a free one which does not.

Boardtracker (http://www.boardtracker.com/) is another forum metasearch engine, but one that draws its results from a different range of sources to those above. Its results include a helpful pie chart showing proportionally where your results have come from, around the globe. Slightly less helpfully, there is no option to filter by country of origin. However, Boardtracker does offer free RSS for search results and an alerts service if you are happy to divulge your email address.

Such general ways of scouring forums are helpful in conventional news sourcing, but many journalists will have her own particular spread of interests and specialisms – so it is always a good idea to find and then routinely access forums in your beat.

For example, if you write on education, you will want to follow Teacherstalk (http://www.teacherstalk.co.uk/). If you are a home-affairs correspondent, you will want to keep an eye on UKpoliceonline (http://www.teacherstalk.co.uk/). If you are a generalist reporter and a parenting issue arises one morning, Mumsnet (http://www.mumsnet.com/) will be worth scouring for potential contributors. There may be many other forums and blogs which will be relevant to you, but which may not be easy to find. One good way to find more relevant sources is to take advantage of Google's *related:* function. For every relevant forum you can find, perform a *related:* search on the domain to eke out more relevant sources, like this:

related:ukpoliceonline.co.uk

Google Blog search (http://blogsearch.google.com/) is also a useful place to dig out forum discussions – include the term *forum* in these searches.

Blogs

As with most online sources, it is best to build up and maintain a list of individuals whose interests (or area) is relevant to your beat. Additionally, it is important to track references to your beat from across the blogosphere.

Several blog search verticals are available, though some in the search community have long decried a general malaise across this field (Smarty, 2008). Technorati (http://technorati.com/) is perhaps one of the longest established means of searching the blogosphere. Their advanced search (http://technorati.com/search?advanced) offers some useful options, such as searching by category and filtering by blog authority (Technorati's own measurement). In reality though (and at the time of writing), minimal UK content is available via this engine.

Google Blog search (http://blogsearch.google.co.uk/) is a high-profile alternative. Though it has far more UK content available, the advanced search is in some ways less utilitarian than Technorati's (especially with regard to ranking results by *authority*). It can be flaky – searching within the UK index would not prevent sites referring to non-UK place names being returned, so it may be necessary to include negative references to related place names from outside the UK. In addition, the index is more generally fully of forums and listings sites (especially property and cars) which can crowd out local or topical news sources. To remove forums posts and listings, it is best to include the term 'blog' in your search – somewhat counter-intuitive given that this is a blog vertical. There is no way to filter out non-UK content and references, so the best hope is to include the term 'UK' in searches. A search for *'cambridge UK-MA'*... will filter out most references to Cambridge Massachusetts (often abbreviated to MA), though perhaps at the expense of material which is not tagged with the term 'UK'.

Unfortunately there are no 'similar' options in Google Blog search results pages. When you find an appropriate blog, and want to find others like it, Google Blog search is probably not the best answer. It is probably easiest to browse down the related links options on the blog in question, but for a more robust approach, try searching for the blog in Open Site Explorer (account required) to unearth other blogs linking to it, which may be related.

Google's main index also has potential in blog search. For subject or beat-specific blogs, run a search including the term 'blog' (i.e. *middlesbrough blog*), then refine using the Pages from the UK filter from the search options panel on the left of the results page (you may need to click on the *More search options* link to drop this option down). For more blogs like the one you have discovered, seek out the *Similar* option under the search result.

Twingly (http://www.twingly.com/search) provides another alternative blog (and social media) search. Their search results pages offer a spam-free filter under the *Any source* option at the top of results pages, but this will not help you deal with the avalanche of listings and jobs pages which are returned – neither will incorporating the term *blog* into your search.

Of all the blog search verticals available, perhaps Blog Pulse (http://blogpulse.com/) offers the most. In this engine, an advanced search (see option on top right of screen) for *'cambridge NOT MA'* ... returns page after page of UK specific, fresh blog results, and an RSS feed for every search too. Their conversation tracker (http://blogpulse.com/conversation) vertical also permits the tracing of debate around your keywords across several popular online news sources and blogs.

Provenance is an ongoing issue in blog search, which from time to time inspires authors to provide tips and source which may help (Schofield, 2008). Finding new blogs local to your interests (especially in the UK) can be difficult and time consuming. It does not help that most blogging platforms go with a .com upper-level domain (rather than .co.uk), nor that some blogs do not include detailed nor standardised biographical information.

Social bookmarking

Most web users are used to bookmarking or saving useful sites and sources once they have found them – it is a crucial part of keeping a grip on research, of making sense of the mass of online content available at our finger tips – and it is also a process which connects all stages of newsgathering into an interconnected chain: from finding sources to publishing them. Saving these resources in the cloud online (making them accessible anywhere, at any time) and sharing them in a social context (where other users can join together in knowledge networks) can help connect journalist, story and audience by exploiting what Halavais calls 'social remembering' (Halavais, 2009, p. 167).

The most popular site which allows this kind of knowledge sharing is Delicious (http://www.delicious.com/) (formerly del.icio.us). This social bookmarking site, which allows its users to create its structure, represents the most efficient way to get a grip of the content you have found online. Because it is platform independent, it allows you to access your saved (or favourite) websites from anywhere – which is useful where you are hot-desking, using one or more home computer or using a mobile in addition to desktop computers – without the hassle of uploading your bookmarks to all the machines you use in the routine of your work.

It is a good idea to use bookmarklets (http://www.delicious.com/help/bookmarklets) to help speed up the process of saving, describing and tagging bookmarks. If you are concerned about privacy, you can mark your saves 'private' using a tick box on the 'save a bookmark' page. Being a social network, you can also share bookmarks with colleagues and friends using the *Network* option. The site can help you both audit a topic or beat, and keep on top of it using RSS.

But you do not need a Delicious account to make good use of this source. It is also a great place for newsgathering, and for finding valued sources and material online, because it harnesses the power of social discovery. You can surf those sites people actually value, you can measure this value by the volume of people who have saved a particular site, and you can isolate every individual who has saved this site establish what you have in common and effectively browse their saves and follow future saves (or particular tags, or search terms) to keep on top of discoveries in your field as time goes on.

You can either search all of Delicious using the search box, focus on particular tags *Explore a tag* (http://www.delicious.com/tag/) or even find a particular web address using the 'Look up a url' (http://www.delicious.com/url/) option. Search results indicate the number of people who have saved each link and the tags used to describe them. Click on the number of users and you can access the full list – however, Delicious user profiles are often less populated than profiles in other sites, and usernames rarely give away who the saver in question is. RSS feeds are available for all types of search results.

Although a timeline is provided in search results, there is no way to sort results by the date they were saved – the default format is by relevance (based on keywords found in titles, notes and tags). There are many add-ons, plugins, extensions and other Delicious-based tools available, some of which offer benefits in search. But Delicious is no cure-all for search – people do not always tag content in a useful or consistent way (if at all), and indeed some have questioned the value of links people save, arguing that an arms-race informs behaviour with people pursuing personal popularity and 'authority' online. Since it was sold by Yahoo in April 2011, some users have migrated elsewhere. But for now, it still contains a significant reach of curated material.

Delicious is not the only social bookmarking tool available for use in online research. Since March 2010, Google Bookmarks have been experimenting with public lists (https://www.google.com/bookmarks/). Though less popular than Delicious, Google Bookmarks (which requires a Google account to access) does index the entire page of your bookmarks, which gives more control and more options in searching those bookmarks which have been shared publicly, while lessening the impact of inaccurate or inconsistent tagging.

Blinklist (http://blinklist.com/) offers an alternative search option, albeit one with relatively little UK content, and lacking much of the functionality found in Delicious. Faves (http://faves.com/SampleProfile.aspx) contains a good deal of content, but does not have a big userbaser. Likewise, social annotation tool like Diigo (http://www.diigo.com/) (which incorporates FURL – account required) may be a useful alternative. CiteULike (http://www.citeulike.org/home) and Connotea (http://www.connotea.org/) offer an academic take on social bookmarking and can both be useful accompaniments to Google Scholar for digging out expertise or esoteric research.

Real-time news aggregators

Traditional search engines are good for finding structured, fixed, archived information, but they have tended to have a blind spot when it comes to indexing and presenting breaking news. Shrewd independent developers spotted a potentially lucrative niche in the market, and so the major search providers have had to play catch-up.

Real-time aggregators are a particularly useful place to watch news as it breaks – though there is some disagreement about a working definition of the term. For the purpose of newsgathering (and the tools introduced here), it is useful to think of real-time news as online media, whether status update, tweet, breaking news story or even links to recently published material, which is published and indexed (and so available to view on appropriate platforms) near instantly.

Social Mention (http://socialmention.com/) is one such platform. Styling itself as a 'social media search engine' more than a real-time search tool, its primary focus is on many of those sources which fuel some of the other engines mentioned here. It is perhaps one of the most far-reaching of all the real-time engines available – indeed it goes far beyond mere breaking news to offer a depth of perspective via many social sites. Though it provides a smattering of trending topics on the homepage, the real value in this service lies in the various means provided to filter and isolate information needs. Once results are returned, it is possible to filter by adding more (commonly found) keywords or by isolating the usernames of those who have contributed most using your keywords. Social Mention draws from a range of multi-media sources, listed conveniently on the left-hand-side navigation in search results. There is real depth to this service and an archive which few competitors can equal.

IceRocket's (http://www.icerocket.com/) Big Buzz vertical (selected from the top right of the search bar) provides timely results organised around different social media strands: blogs, Twitter, Facebook status updates, video, news and images. Twitter results show how many followers a poster has, though Facebook updates do not. All text-based results tell you how recently they were posted, and it is worth noting that news results do not discriminate between local, national, international, old- and new-media sources. A downside to using this tool is that it is very search dependent – the *Buzzing searches* on IceRocket's home page are fairly inappropriate for hard news journalism.

There are several means of keeping on top of Twitter in real time. Twingly live (http://live.twingly.com/) offers a means of setting up rolling real-time search results, incorporating as many (or as few) keywords as is appropriate to your subject area. Results offer a preview of links so you can detect spam, which, at the time of writing, is a pervasive problem in real-time search.

Twittorati (http://twittorati.com/) brings the worlds of blogging and microblogging together – allowing users to establish followers on Twitter by how highly ranked their respective blogs are. Though it should be noted, those 'bloggers' who comprise the top 100 (as presented on the left-hand column of Twittorati's home page) represent a who's who of the usual suspects in news media and technology. At the time of writing, all the top-ranked political blogs are US based, leaving little scope for those concerned with UK politics.

Topsy (http://topsy.com/) provides yet another alternative. Their experts directory (http://topsy.com/experts) offers a means of seeking out experts by mentions across Twitter, and its depth of archive (dating back to May 2008, at the time of writing) makes it an especially useful tool. Tweetmeme (http://tweetmeme.com/) offers a range of channels, one of which lets you browse through the top news-linked stories by most recent, Top in 24 hours and Top in 7 days as shared across Twitter, though technology stories (and by all accounts self-promotion) tend to crowd out results. Twitturly (http://twitturly.com/) lets you track those links which have prompted so much debate across Twitter, with helpful verticals for news, images and video.

To track big topics and your own bespoke interests in real time, Twitterfall (http://www.twitterfall.com/) provides an elegant and robust solution – so much so that it has been used in industry (Oliver, 2009). Follow general trends, or set up your own rolling feeds via Twitter lists, filter by search, by geolocation or by search logic to construct your own news platform. Both Twitter Advanced search (http://search.twitter.com/advanced) and Geochirp (http://www.geochirp.com/) allow you to limit your search to within 1 kilometre and 1 mile of a postcode or place respectively (the former even supports search by fractions of a mile). As some of these sources develop, and provide a geographically determined means of presenting news by popularity, their utility will surely improve for UK researchers and journalists.

Some other real-time search options include: WhosTalkin (http://whostalkin.com/) and Kurrently (http://www.kurrently.com/).

Finding social search trends

Trends in search have been used in real time to track the spread of disease (http://www.google.org/flutrends/), and historic search trends have even been explored by economists as a means of predicting future economic activity (McLaren, 2011). The use of web trends in newsgathering can be controversial. Some warn that using search trend data as a means of deciding which stories to cover, or chasing traffic associated with some popular trends at the expense of traditional news-gathering methods, can put pressure on journalistic standards and risks freezing out genuine, public interest journalism as a result (Currah, 2009). On the other hand, it may fairly be argued that web trends represent the purist form of demand online – and after all, journalists' role is to give their readers the content they want to read.

By keeping on top of web trends in the newsroom, it is possible to discern what the public are interested in. But the following resources for establishing what is trending can also be used proactively in the newsroom; to inspire original stories, to help journalists make the most of their coverage of a popular issue and to get a sense for how your content matches with global (or local) search demand, outwith the confines of your own in-house analytics tools.

Google Trends UK (http://www.google.co.uk/trends) offers a modest top-10 'Hot Topics' at any given time, which you can compare and contrast with US hot searches (for which, at the time of writing, there are some 20 trending terms listed. You can also search for trends, but these are not UK specific.

Google Insights (http://www.google.com/insights/search/?hl=en-GB#) takes the Google Trends concept further, providing various options for in-depth analysis of internet memes. You can isolate particular verticals (such as News or Images), and regions – a heatmap shows the popularity of terms geographically. Search results include those terms most associated with your terms: both 'top' and 'rising' trends. Only a portion of web traffic across Google's domains is used, which is presented relative to the total number of searches undertaken in Google over time. In terms of analysing your results, it is important to bear in mind that a declining line does not mean absolute traffic for your term is decreasing – just that the overall popularity of this term is decreasing. Google Insights can be a source for news stories, nationally (Warman, 2010) and internationally (Morgan, 2010). But perhaps more conventionally, tools like this can be used to keep tabs on what the surfing public is interested in.

Yahoo!'s Buzz index (http://buzzlog.yahoo.com/buzzlog) represents an interesting (albeit altogether less interactive) alternative to Google's efforts. Published Tuesday to Saturday, this edited list of stories is compiled from trends in Yahoo! Search log files and is updated daily. At the time of writing, there is no UK Buzzlog.

For tracking trends in Twitter there are a broad array of different tools, many freely available. While Twitter's web interface offers personalisable trends (by location), there are many other sources which offer a different approach, more granularity to your coverage, and more options. Once you have logged into your Twitter account via Twitscoop (http://www.twitscoop.com/), for example, you can watch trends come and go using their *Buzzing right now* tag cloud, or by using their interactive timeline.

If you do not know why something is trending and do not have time to search around, What the Trend's UK index can be instructive:

*http://whatthetrend.com/?woeid=23424975&place*_name=United%20 Kingdom

Trendsmap (http://trendsmap.com/) offers a visual means of tracking trends geographically. You can follow trends around your particular location, or a city, and additionally, for those not interested in big conurbations but in the spread of trends across a region, the interactive map offers a *My region* option. This resource is fully interactive, allowing for zoom to varying degrees of granularity, with trends superimposed over the map.

Trendistic (now defunct) used to offer insights into historic Twitter trends. This tool was used to challenge the false assumption that criticism of journalist Jan Moir's controversial *Daily Mail* opinion piece on the death of Steven Gately was drummed up by celebrity tweeter Stephen Fry (Bradshaw, 2009).

As one of the most popular sites on the net, Wikipedia is a key source for tracking online 'buzz'. Trends in Wikipedia activity can be monitored using a number of different sources. Trending Topics (http://www.trendingtopics.org/) provides a list of the most commonly viewed Wikipedia content over the past 30 days, along with a *Rising* (24 hours) option. Content can be viewed according to a number of types, including People and Finance – and near real-time monitoring is available via the current-hour option (http://www.trendingtopics.org/hourly_trends).

Uptrends for topic pages (and associated popular pages) benchmarked over the past 24 hours can be viewed via Wikitrends (http://toolserver.org/~johang/wikitrends/english-uptrends-today.html). Wikirage (http://www.wikirage.com/) provides an overview of the most edited Wikipedia pages – over the past hour, six hours, day, three days, week and month. As for online video, the best way to keep on top of those most viewed, and most popular videos in YouTube, is via their Video channel (http://www.youtube.com/videos?s=mp); here you can browse the past day's, week's or month's content. Several categories are available, including News (http://www.youtube.com/news).

In terms of images, Google/Flickr Zeitgeist (http://fiveprime.org/zeitgeist.html) offers hourly updates of trending search terms, and the images they yield. For music, Next Big Sound (http://www.nextbigsound.com/) lets you see how popular musicians are proving, across those musical areas of the social web (such as Last.fm and Myspace) as well as Facebook, Twitter and Wikipedia. For consumer goods, Amazon's Movers and Shakers (http://www.amazon.com/gp/movers-and-shakers/) shows how popular different products are (including books, music and technology) – which can be a useful source for consumer journalism, and features.

For a very general overview of web-based trends, Trendsbuzz (http://trendsbuzz.com/) is a helpful resource, while SEOMoz popular searches (http://www.seomoz.org/popular-searches) provides a similar overview service across many different sources.

References

Bradshaw, Paul (2009) Notes on #janmoir – don't 'blame' Fry, Online Journalism Blog, October 17: http://onlinejournalismblog.com/2009/10/17/notes-on-janmoir-dont-blame-fry/

Bunz, Mercedes (2009) With its real-time search, Google is creating an archive of the present, The Guardian, December 08: http://www.guardian.co.uk/technology/pda/2009/dec/08/real-time-search-google

Burstein, Paul (2013) 'Now showing: Older Tweets in search results', Official Twitter Blog, Februrary 7: https://blog.twitter.com/2013/now-showing-older-tweets-search-results

Constine, Josh (2012) Where The Ladies At? Pinterest. 2 Million Daily Facebook Users, 97% Of Fans Are Women, TechCrunch, February 11: http://techcrunch.com/2012/02/11/pinterest-stats/

Currah, James (2009) *What's Happening to our News*. Reuters Institute for the Study of Journalism: Oxford.

Galperin, Eva and York, Jillian (2011) Victory! Google Surrenders in the Nymwars, Electronic Frontiers Foundation, October 19: https://www.eff.org/deeplinks/2011/10/victory-google-surrenders-nymwars

Goodman, Eli (2009) What History Tells us About Facebook's Potential as a Search Engine, Part 1, April 26: http://searchenginewatch.com/article/2065524/What-History-Tells-us-About-Facebooks-Potential-as-a-Search-Engine-Part-1

Goad, Robin (2010) Social networks now more popular than search engines in the UK, June 08: http://weblogs.hitwise.com/robin-goad/2010/06/social_networks_overtake_search_engines.html

Halavais, Alexander (2009) *Search Engine Society (Digital Media and Society Series)*. Polity Press: London.

Halfacree, Gareth (2010) Google's Buzz causes privacy concerns, Bit-Tech, February 11: http://www.bit-tech.net/news/bits/2010/02/11/googles-buzz-causes-privacy-concerns/1

Hughes, Nicola (2011) Sorting the Social Media Chaos, Data Miner UK blog, May 30: http://datamineruk.wordpress.com/2011/05/30/sorting-the-social-media-chaos/

Kollewe, Julia (2009) Twitter is not for teens, Morgan Stanley told by 15-year-old expert, The Guardian, July 13: http://www.guardian.co.uk/business/2009/jul/13/twitter-teenage-media-habits

McLaren, Nick (2011) Using Internet Search Data as economic indicators, Bank of England Quarterly Bulletin, Q2: http://www.bankofengland.co.uk/publications/quarterlybulletin/qb110206.pdf

Morgan, Kelli (2010) No. 1 Nation in Sexy Web Searches? Call it Pornistan, Fox News, July 13: http://www.foxnews.com/world/2010/07/12/data-shows-pakistan-googling-pornographic-material/#ixzz1PpQap5Aq

Myslewski, Rik (2010) Facebook tops half-billion users, wants your innermost thoughts, The Register, July 21: http://www.theregister.co.uk/2010/07/21/facebook_tops_billion_active_users/

Nielsen Wire (2009) The More Affluent and More Urban are More Likely to use Social Networks, September 25: http://blog.nielsen.com/nielsenwire/online_mobile/the-more-affluent-and-more-urban-are-more-likely-to-use-social-networks/

Oliver, Laura (2009) 'Twitterfall makes it onto Telegraph newsroom screens', Journalism.co.uk. February 25: http://blogs.journalism.co.uk/2009/02/25/twitterfall-makes-it-onto-telegraph-newsroom-screens/

Perez, Sarah (2009) Ten ways to archive your tweets, Read Write Web, August 11: http://www.readwriteweb.com/archives/10_ways_to_archive_your_tweets.php

Royal Pingdom (2009) Study: Males vs. females in social networks, Royal Pingdom, November 27: http://royal.pingdom.com/2009/11/27/study-males-vs-females-in-social-networks/

Royal Pingdom (2010) Study: Ages of social network users, Royal Pingdom, February 16: http://royal.pingdom.com/2010/02/16/study-ages-of-social-network-users/

Schofield, Jack (2008) Searching blogs by location, The Guardian, August 28: http://www.guardian.co.uk/technology/askjack/2008/aug/28/searchingblogsbylocation

Schroeder, Stan (2009) Facebook Users Are Getting Older. Much Older, Mashable, July 07: http://mashable.com/2009/07/07/facebook-users-older/

Smarty, Ann (2008) Blog Search Engines : The Complete Overview, Search Engine Journal, September 28: http://www.searchenginejournal.com/blog-search-engines-the-complete-overview/7856/

Social Media Optimisation (2008) Social Network User Demographics, May 29: http://social-media-optimization.com/2008/05/social-network-user-demographics/

Sparrow, Andrew (2009) Twitter users: young, metropolitan and angry about civil liberties, The Guardian, November 18: http://www.guardian.co.uk/technology/2009/nov/18/twitter-users-survey-poll-britain

Su, Susan (2010 Who's Using Facebook Around the World? The Demographics of Facebook's Top 15 Country Markets, Inside Facebook, June 08: http://www.insidefacebook.com/2010/06/08/whos-using-facebook-around-the-world-the-demographics-of-facebooks-top-15-country-markets/

Van Grove (2010) Bing Adds Facebook Updates and Links to Search Results, Mashable, June 09: http://mashable.com/2010/06/09/bing-adds-facebook/

Warman, Matthew (2010) General Election 2010: the Google trends during the leaders' debate, The Telegraph, April 16: http://www.telegraph.co.uk/news/election-2010/7597345/General-Election-2010-the-Google-trends-during-the-leaders-debate.html

Wasserman, Todd (2012) Larry Page: Google+ Now Has 90 Million Users, Mashable, January 19: http://mashable.com/2012/01/19/google-plus-90-million/

6 Multimedia

Introduction

Few web users would struggle to name some common sources for finding video, images and audio online. But finding such material as a means of sourcing or substantiating news in a timely way is an altogether more taxing matter.

Legal and ethical factors in the use of multimedia online

Time constraints are not the only pressure journalists experience in finding and selecting online multimedia – legal and ethical issues abound too. Those responsible for creating multimedia which appears online retain rights over these items – so it behoves any journalist wishing to use such material to contact the author in order to request permission for use. If this is not possible, the journalist runs a risk of legal action, and while the law of fair use may be available to counter strictures in intellectual property rights in some situations (where applied to small portions of text for example), such use could nonetheless lead to legal action. In any event, fair use does not apply to all media – photography is exempt under UK definition of the concept (Banks and Hanna, 2009, p. 452). Where a third-party image is used to identify someone in the public eye, the public interest defence in using this image without permission may be stronger than where an image is merely decorative. But intellectual property rights are not the only legal barrier to using multimedia. Where a journalist does not factor in the running of active legal proceedings, the publication of multimedia evidence that may incriminate someone, or bias someone's legal position, can lead to action under contempt laws.

The issue of ethics in handling social media explored in Chapter 4 applies equally to the use of multimedia found therein – as does the issue of taste and decency (whether in the form of industry regulation, or in-house media best practice, and guidance). In very simple terms, it is therefore necessary for journalists to avail themselves of best practice, regulatory regimes and the criminal and civil laws of the domain in which they are working before setting out to use multimedia found online in their published journalism.

Here follows a range of sources to help find multimedia online.

Finding video

Today YouTube (http://www.youtube.com/) has grown in scale so much that it can be difficult to find content by means of conventional search. To help, the site offers filters and ordering preferences when your search results are returned; it also supports some Boolean search, and some Google advanced operators too, including phrase searching, the wildcard keyword placeholder (*) and the *intitle:* command. Search aside, there are other methods which can help filter results. For example, it is possible to fast forward or rewind to a specific point in minutes and seconds within a YouTube video by appending some code to the end of the URL: *#t=05m30s* (where #t=XXmZZs with XX representing minutes and ZZ seconds). This can be useful for sharing content hidden in long videos.

YouTube's chart option (http://www.youtube.com/charts) allows you to see what are the most popular, trending videos at any time. This can be fairly limited, not least due to the inconsistent (and sometime incorrect) way some people categorise their videos, but also due to the heavy US bias of content sourced this way. For these reasons, it is perhaps best to refer to the 'most' options, rather than subject-specific content. YouTube's categories page (http://www.youtube.com/videos) offers (at the times of writing) the same content in an alternative layout.

While RSS feeds are available for categories in YouTube, it is a little-known fact that RSS feeds for keywords (or tags) are also available, if you are prepared to do some URL hacking:

http://gdata.youtube.com/feeds/videos/-/

Simply copy the above URL into a browser and replace *keyword>* with your tag of choice. If you would like to set up a feed for more than one keyword, put a forward slash after the first, and then type out the second.

Downloading YouTube videos is a precarious business in terms of copyright, and for the purpose of newsgathering (or sharing information), it is not necessary. But it is possible via a range of third-party operators, and some browsers. In addition to YouTube, Google Videos (http://video.google.co.uk/) aggregates content from several online video providers in one place. It shares the same search syntax as YouTube, and RSS feeds can be obtained by scrolling to the bottom of results, selecting 'Create an email alert for…', then selecting the 'feed' option in the Deliver to menu.

Blinkx (http://www.blinkx.com/) aggregates less content than Truveo (concentrating mostly on ITN and Press Association content), and as such suffers in terms of up-to-datedness. Nevertheless, it does offer a news category which provides the day's news in summary (http://www.blinkx.com/topics/news).

When it comes to searching the videos shared in social media, Viddler (http://www.viddler.com/) is a good starting place. As far as media shared across just Twitter is concerned, Twitvid (http://www.twitvid.com/) can be useful, albeit the search interface is minimal; you can not order results by time, let alone get an RSS feed from them.

Veoh (http://www.veoh.com/), a US-based aggregator, pulls together content from major film and TV production companies, independents and members of the public. The News section (http://www.veoh.com/list/videos/news) offers a means of tracking stories as they break, albeit only by language used (spoken, and in subtitles). There is a significant US bias, and few UK broadcasters have channels, which can equally be said for Daily Motion (http://www.dailymotion.com), despite its UK filter. Clipblast (http://clipblast.com) offers a more UK-friendly service, while Vimeo (http://www.vimeo.com) is more concerned with hosting amateur content (with, again, a significant US bias).

Other social (and streaming) video services worthy of mention include:

Metacafe (http://www.metacafe.com/)
Videosurf (metasearch engine) (http://www.videosurf.com/)

In addition, there are many, many more video streaming sites (such as Hulu) which, for contractual reasons, require a US IP address to access.

A perfectly valid means of sourcing news, UK broadcasters have their own (limited) on-demand services online, which include:

BBC iPlayer (http://www.bbc.co.uk/iplayer/)
Sky Player (http://skyplayer.sky.com/vod/page/default/home.do)
4od (http://www.channel4.com/programmes/4od)
TVCatchup (http://www.tvcatchup.com/)

There are also several streaming services (aside from relative latecomers YouTube, Google+ and Facebook), including Livestream (http://www.livestream.com/) and Ustream (http://www.ustream.tv/).

Lastly, for sourcing older video archive, here are some useful professional (many of them subscription) sites:

Art Beats (http://www.artbeats.com/)
BBC Motion Gallery (http://www.bbcmotiongallery.com/)
Footage.net (http://www.footage.net/)
Free Stock Footage (http://www.freestockfootage.com/)
ITN Archive (http://www.itnsource.com/)
MovieTone (http://www.movietone.com/)

Finding images

Image search can inform several functions in journalism, from sparking ideas (creative thinking), to newsgathering, to (more conventionally) sourcing images to publish with written content. In terms of these first two categories of user need, there are many free alternatives from which to choose.

Google Images (http://www.google.co.uk/imghp) remains the best mass-market image search engine available across the web. Its index far surpasses its nearest rivals, and it has become more utilitarian since it enabled reverse-image search, introduced in October 2011. This is a particularly useful tool for verifying images, and ensuring that images claimed to be original are not already in the public domain – as covered in a later chapter. Google's image results are more 'social' today than they were, by means of the *Google+* option. The assumptions driving Google's quest to bring ever-increasing 'relevance' is tightening up their understanding of the intent behind search queries.

Exalead images (http://www.exalead.com/search/image/) works across a much smaller collection, of what are generally non-UK specific results (which are also less likely to come from social media accounts). All of Exalead's advanced operators can be used (at least in theory) in its image search. This platform offers an advanced operator which allows searchers looking for images of people to filter results by only bringing back 'face' shots (either select the option, or key in *imagecontent:Face* in addition to your search terms). However, unlike Google Images, Exalead will not auto-correct your search terms – so finding images of *Muhamed Quaddafi* (and the multiple ways in which his name was spelled) is not as straightforward as it could be.

Image and video hosting site Flickr has an emphasis much more on sharing content, than on professional photography (albeit there are many professionals and freelancers who publish their photography on the site). Flickr (along with del.icio.us) was an early pioneer of the 'folksonomy', encouraging the use of indexing based on bottom-up tagging by members, rather than top-down indexing by 'experts', or automated systems. As such, it can be more intuitive to use (depending on what words and language you share with other users), but equally it can be rather hit-and-miss (with inconsistent and incorrect indexing in some images, which would not necessarily be corrected by someone else in the Flickr community).

Flickr's advanced search (http://www.flickr.com/search/advanced/) is particularly useful in terms of sourcing fresh, original and easy-to-clear content. Besides offering search by update (which can be useful for news events), it also offers a checkbox which can be used to limit results to images with a Creative Commons license, which are both easier to clear and usually free to use (so long as credit is given) in news journalism – and so which are preferable to the time-intensive process of tracking a copyright-holder down and negotiating permissions.

It should be noted that there are some limitations with Flickr's RSS options; despite claiming to offer RSS for photostreams, group & forum discussions and specific tags, surfers may struggle to find these options for all content. Fortunately, there are some third-party alternatives, such as DeGreave's Flickr RSS Feed Generator (http://www.degraeve.com/), which can be used to set up feeds by date order (descending) for any Flickr tag. Fiveprime's Google/Flickr Zeitgeist (http://fiveprime.org/zeitgeist.html) is another hugely useful third-party add-on for tapping into trends in pictures shared on Flickr.

Flickr has a number of competitors in the field of user-generated images, not least:

Instagram (http://instagram.com/)
Picasa (http://picasaweb.google.com)
Panoramio (http://www.panoramio.com/) and
Photobucket (http://photobucket.com/findstuff/)

In May 2011, Twitter launched its own photo-sharing services, but there remain several alternatives such as:

Twicsy (http://twicsy.com/) (offers search-based RSS)
Twitpic (http://twitpic.com/)
Yfrog (http://yfrog.com/)

There are also engines which allow viewing of images shared on Twitter in a real-time flow, such as Picfog (http://picfog.com/), Twitcaps (http://twitcaps.com/) and Pingwire for mobile (http://pingwire.com/). These search engines can be a good way to filter out non-visual tweets; and can be worked into real-time news-gathering system. But equally, they often contain material which is not safe for work.

If you plan to use images you have found online in your work, it is essential to make sure you have the permission of the rights-holder to use them. This is where Creative Commons content comes in useful. It is possible to filter advanced Google image results by usage rights, but there are also bespoke verticals which can help here, including:

Creative Commons image search (http://creativecommons.org/ image/)Everystockphoto (http://www.everystockphoto.com/ index.php)

Clearing multimedia for use online can be an expensive process, especially if there is no Creative Commons license available. But if you have a working budget, there are a number of premium services which offer stock photography, which journalists may avail themselves of, including:

Corbis Images Royalty Free (http://www.corbisimages.com/stock-photo/royalty-free/)
Gettyimages royalty free (http://www.gettyimages.co.uk /CreativeImages/RoyaltyFree)
British Pathe Stills archive (http://www.britishpathe.com/)

For an exhaustive list of image sources see here:

http://randomknowledge.wordpress.com/2008/05/09/how-to-find-images-on-the-internet/

Finding music

Aside from iTunes (http://www.apple.com/itunes/) and Spotify (http://www.spotify.com/uk/), there are many other places to find and listen to music online, including:

Dogpile (http://www.dogpile.com/) (check the Audio filter)
Metacrawler (http://www.metacrawler.co.uk/) (check the Audio filter)

Mixcloud (http://www.mixcloud.com/) (especially good for playlists)
Soundcloud (http://soundcloud.com/)

In terms of recommendations, Amazon's listmania is particularly useful, albeit they can also be a little contrived. Blip.fm and Last.fm both offer more intuitive recommendations.

There are also several sources online for finding audio and 'podcasts':

AudioBoo (http://audioboo.fm/)
Twaudio (http://twaud.io/)
Chirbit (www.chirbit.com/)

Using Google's *filetype:* extension (covered earlier in this book) can also be useful in this field, where you refine by audio filetypes. Using free-text search to find appropriate music for your package can throw up some interesting surprises; it can be helpful (and serendipitous) way of adding a touch of levity to your package. Google's domain filter (*site:*), when used to search across the domains of particular file-sharing sites (like Rapidshare, Zshare or Megaupload), can also yield useful results.

If you do not have the money, time or patience to clear commercial music, there is no shortage of Production music (or 'mood music') companies online, where you can find suitable music to accompany your productions. Of course opinion is divided over the editorial value of this type of music (some believe it to be emotionally manipulative and crass); however, be aware that there are options out there:

Arcadia (http://www.arcadiamusic.com/) (account required)
Dewolfe (http://www.dewolfe.co.uk/)
Extreme (http://www.extrememusic.com/)
Sonoton (http://www.sonoton.com/)
Universal Publishing Production Music (http://www.unippm.com/)

Finding Sound effects is fairly straightforward online, but clearance can be more complicated than music or TV archive. Many of these sites are amateur, and there is no guarantee that you would not stumble across material which has been lifted from others – so you may want to state your intentions with the Webmaster of the site you find them on:

Find Sounds (http://www.findsounds.com/)
Sounddogs (http://www.sounddogs.com/)

Alternatively, you can take a mini disk or MP3 recorder to the British Library Sound Archive, which is located at:

Sound Archive Information Service
The British Library
Sound Archive
96 Euston Road
London
NW1 2DB
United Kingdom
Tel: +44 (0)20 7412 7831
Fax: +44 (0)20 7412 7691

Reference

Banks, David and Hanna, Mark (2009) *McNae's Essential Law for Journalists.* Oxford: Oxford University Press.

7 Bringing it all together: developing an online beat

The beat in a networked world

The concept of the 'beat' has a rich lexical history; an early etymological manifestation comes from the field of navigation in the form of 'beating the bounds', meaning 'to trace out boundaries in a perambulation, certain objects in the line of journey being formally struck, and sometimes also boys whipped to make them remember' (MacDonald, 1977, p. 113). Its application to journalism today has shed most of the masochism; it can best be summarised as 'the routine path and set of locations that a reporter will visit each day, which brings them into contact with organisations that produce such news events' (Machin and Niblock, 2006, p. 72).

Fishman (1980), concerned with newsgathering in crime journalism, concluded that the news schedule (which demands a regular and consistent flow of information and stories) encourages journalistic dependence upon bureaucratic entities: councils, police forces, hospitals and other 'official' sources. The routinisation of newsgathering around these sources help journalists plan and prioritise the news (Harrison, 2006, p. 141), and bestow authority upon news output, taking the form of 'objective' sources of information (Tuchman, 1972), but at a cost (Foreman, 2010), for it leads to cynicism and disillusionment among audiences, as talking heads become evermore distanced from the communities they serve (Carey, 1999).

The ritualisation of newsgathering and news sourcing is driven by a series of symbiotic and consensual processes wherein journalist and source both gain. Exploration of this sustenance of mutual dependence permeates much early literature in this field (Zelizer, 2004). McManus argues that our media thrive as an active arbiter within a market, bartering 'access to the public to news sources in return for information needed to fill the paper or newscast' (McManus, 1994, p. 5). But non-institutional organisations can take advantage of the diminution

111

of editorial resources found in many modern newsrooms too (Davis, 2000); this is a market in which material wealth is not all that matters – social capital is a recognised currency too.

The beat is culturally relative; it does not exist in an hermetically sealed bubble. Commercial pressures shape it, and, some argue, threatened its very existence. During the mid-1990s, topic teams emerged in US media, replacing beat reporters and uncoupling the ties between local audiences and journalists – something many journalists of the era consider to be to journalism's detriment (Hansen et al., 1998). In the UK, the 1990s saw the rise of new technologies and marketing strategies, reinforcing the dominance of official voices in news. Industry consolidation (and resultant job cuts) impacted the beat. Fewer journalists began covering long-established geographical beats, work became consolidated around regional hubs and removed from local communities. The job cuts presaged a flight of journalists into public relations, who, in turn, began to feed those time-poor journalists who remain with easy-to-assemble news copy (Machin and Niblock, 2006, p. 70).

In the UK today, local beats are coming under pressure. Although local government data is available in unparalleled quantities, political decision-making (framed by the Local Government Act 2000), is more opaque than the committee system it replaced (Morrison, 2010). The rise of the council newspaper 'propaganda sheets', which are a competitive threat to local newspapers (Gilligan, 2009) may have abated, but the sweeping reforms promised before the 2010 election have not materialised (Department for Communities and Local Government, 2011). Another key 'beat' source, court reporting, is considered to be in decline, and certainly some newspaper groups struggle to justify it on cost-benefits analysis, leaving police forces to do a key job reporters used to do (BBC News, 2011).

In the early 1990s, 'public journalism' (or 'civic journalism') emerged as an alternative to the corporate-driven model which had swept away all before it in the American media market. Here was an attempt to de-institutionalise the profession. The rituals and practices concerning private (and protected) relationships in the old 'beat' were considered reactionary, standing counter to the public interest. The old relationships and routines which tie journalists to their beat were conceived of as a conspiracy against the people. The trust we place in our government has plummeted, as has the trust we place in their news media, leading to further experimentation with new journalistic forms and means of engagement with the audience (Haas, 2003; Haas and Steiner, 2006).

Today we can look back on the burgeoning re-emergence of these experiments in online journalism, in the context of the rise of the network society. Nodes in the network are not of equal importance, and, indeed, power relations are determined by inclusion or exclusion from the network (Castells, 2000, p. 15). This is problematic for public interest journalism insofar as social networks do not proportionally reflect wider society in terms of engagement or use – only one in 20 of those over 65 engage with social media frequently, and less than a third of 35–44 year-olds are active online (Ofcom, 2010). When it comes to news-gathering online to developing sources, and reaching out to audiences, journalists must be careful how their networks develop, for pluralism is risked in an exclusively online network.

The rise of the network in online journalism, evidenced in everything from crowdsourcing via Twitter to the processing of User Generated Content in the form multimedia, offers a means of extending public interest journalism, and of re-inventing the 'beat'. The network potential within the Internet can help bring about the re-constitution of journalism's traditional power base, re-connecting journalists with their audience online within a wider social network.

Establishing an online beat

Aside from the search engines and social networks covered earlier, there are a range of bespoke verticals journalists (and news audiences) can use to access the news. Here follows a detailed look at some of the most useful by function.

News search verticals

Google News (http://news.google.co.uk/) offers a relatively small number of generic news subject categories, but it is possible to create bespoke categories using Custom Sections:

http://news.google.com/news/directory/createsection?cf=all&hl=en

This can be useful for journalists and other information professionals working in conceptual (or even geographical) beats, albeit it is not necessarily something the wider public shows any great demand for (Thurman, 2011).

Google News used to publicise the fact that it indexed 25,000 sources worldwide (with 4,500 news sources from the UK), but no official list is available, and indeed these figures have been disputed (Jarboe, 2007).

The fact that many of these sources provide direct public relations copy has led some to question the blurring of lines between editorial and PR in online news aggregation (Orlowski, 2003).

Google News provides an advanced interface, and a range of filters including source, country, and byline. Headline search is available from the *Occurrences* drop-down. It is possible to search more than one location in Google News, but not from the advanced search panel. To do this, you must use the operator location: in an OR search, so, for example,

"Celtic" location:Ireland

...will return results mentioning Celtic exclusively from this country (i.e. search results will be sourced from publications within the country specified). In some searches, this can help filter out irrelevant content (the above search likely won't return results about the *Boston Celtics*). Results can be ranked by date or relevance and results for major news stories are generally clustered (the source of much competition among online news publishers, vying for top position in the cluster). Search results are available in RSS or email-alert formats. Google News contains only around 30 days worth of news, and most journalists will require access to much deeper archives available elsewhere.

Yahoo News (http://uk.news.yahoo.com/) offers a much more developed, hierarchical range of default categories than Google News does, but far, far fewer sources (it is unclear precisely how many). One fundamental difference between Yahoo News and Google News is that the former includes news published by Yahoo. It is important to use Yahoo News in addition to Google News not only because of differences in indexing and coverage, but also to offset any bias in results (Google News search results have proven to be more partisan compared with sources found in Yahoo News) (Ulken, 2005).

The advanced search options (http://search.news.yahoo.com/ advanced) permit filtering by source and country. Bing offers a UK news category too (http://www.bing.com/news/) which has potential for news search.

Google News, Yahoo News and Bing News are all conventional search verticals, and functionality for each is optimised for searchers who know what they are looking for. But for some search needs, searching is neither optimal nor sometimes even possible. This is where other approaches are useful, such as browsing. This injects the potential for the sort of serendipity we experience when browsing newspapers into search, and can be a much more intuitive way of sourcing news than search.

Newsnow (http://www.newsnow.co.uk/), with its easily browsed (and detailed) hierarchy of topics, embodies this approach. Newsnow is more of a news directory than a search engine, and its up-to-date (and densely populated) hierarchy of topics offer an intuitive touch, facilitating use in a very different way to the folksonomies found in some multimedia platforms. It is possible to search Newsnow, but only for one keyword at a time (for free), as using any more than one keyword will incur a charge. Some of the bigger UK news publishers have blocked Newsnow from indexing their content, but it remains a key resource for any local beat journalist.

Most online journalists will be familiar with seeing icons for...

Digg (http://digg.com/),
reddit (http://www.reddit.com/),
Stumbleupon (http://www.stumbleupon.com/)

...and other news sharing (or social news) sites peppered all around their copy. But there can be more to these sites than merely a means of distributing news; all of them aggregate news from around the web, making it easy to catch up on what online audiences are most interested in.

It is argued that the front page of Digg, where the inclusion and arrangement of stories is determined by its users (via an algorithm), represents a means of sampling 'what is interesting today?' (Halavais, 2009, p. 165). However, as with any statistical sample, skewing is possible. The popularity of content trending on these sites should always be taken with a pinch of salt as some politically motivated groups have been found to mobilise and effectively censor material they do not like on Digg (Halliday, 2010). For those who tire of visiting and re-visiting these social news sites, Popurls (http://popurls.com/) offers a trending list for each of them and more, presenting them in a relatively lo-fi, and unassuming way.

It has been argued that news verticals such as Google News assume journalistic functions (Machill et al., 2005), especially with regard to editorialisation on home pages, and ranking content by 'relevance'. It could also be argued that the format of conventional search engines does not lend itself well to different interpretations of the news. For these reasons, it is important for plurality in newsgathering, not to rely too much on one particular form of interface, or one way of interacting with search results.

As an alternative to the ten-results-in-a-list approach to new search engines, Silobreaker (http://www.silobreaker.com/) offers a unique news-gathering experience. Silobreaker is a semantic search engine; it understands key concepts in the news, insofar as it allows them to be isolated from the rest of news text. The service comprises news content which is filtered by a conventional search algorithm, but in conjunction with a community-constructed directory (or thesaurus) of names and concepts in the news. The Hotspots option (found along the top of the search bar) is one of the few remaining places online where geo-coded news can be found in (visual) map form. The 'Network' option makes use of a thesaurus (or 'wiki') of proper nouns and descriptors, presenting the searcher with a social network diagram of all the companies, people, organisations, cities, key phrases and products which feature alongside your area of interest in the news. This is an excellent way to 'audit' news around key people/elements in the news to ensure you have not missed anything. This is just not possible in conventional search results.

Generic news aggregation – the news palate

Just as iGoogle offers a means of personalising web experience, so too are there various engines which offer an equivalent experience for news. Addictomatic (http://addictomatic.com/) encourages surfers to type in a keyword and 'inhale' the web; it presents results from various verticals (spanning multimedia, blogs, social media and news) in one convenient place.

There are a number of other services which offer a similar news palate, albeit focusing on textual, conventional news, rather than multimedia and social media. Ensembli (account required) (http://ensembli.com/) offers a more linear, text-based news offering, and one for which there are far fewer timely results, but nevertheless its uncomplicated interface has benefits.

EU Feeds (http://www.eufeeds.eu/) offers the latest ten stories from key media for EU countries, coverage from all of which can be increased or decreased according to taste. This service is offered for all EU countries, state by state, organised by tab across the top of the page. For newspaper front pages, the imaginatively titled Front Pages Today (http://www.frontpagestoday.co.uk/) offers an overview of the UK nationals, while Newseum (http://www.newseum.org/todaysfrontpages/) sources international news titles (selection is more exploratory than comprehensive).

Daylife's topics (http://www.daylife.com/topics) offer a limited entry-point into current global (albeit dominated by the US) news themes. News is arranged around conventional topics and the people/entities hitting the headlines within them. Pictorial stories tend to dominate, unsurprisingly given Daylife's business interests are closely aligned with those of Getty Images. Newser (http://www.newser.com/) offers an aesthetically appealing artist's palate view of the news (called 'the grid'). This user-curated aggregator shows what was trending on days in months gone by, though US news dominates (again). Newsvine (http://www.newsvine.com/) offers an easy-to-use social search news experience, albeit one which is severely limited if you are interested in a UK geographical beat – though several cities are covered, very few contributors specialise at this level of specificity. Newsvine (http://www.newsvine.com/) and Buzztracker (http://www.buzztracker.com/) offer alternatives, but both are US-centric in their coverage.

Automated news: email alerts

The search engines and aggregators introduced so far in this chapter can be classified as 'pull' technologies; that is, they pull the surfer towards them in order to satisfy search needs. All of them serve a purpose as far as accessing a range of news sources is concerned; albeit it can be time-consuming and frustrating having to go back to each in turn as part of a regular routine, even more so when following a breaking news story. To complement newsgathering, and add system to the process, it can be useful to set up 'push' technologies, like email alerts, which are not so time-consuming.

Google Alerts UK (http://www.google.co.uk/alerts) (registration required) are the most comprehensive way of keeping up on keyword mentions across the Internet. These alerts are more customisable than the services' competitors, taking advantage of the speciality verticals Google excels in (including news, blogs and video search). It is possible to set the frequency of these alerts to weekly, daily or as they occur – but of course this could quickly lead to a saturated email inbox. Boolean logic and some advanced operators (including the *site:* function) are supported in Google Alerts. There is an important caveat attached to alert results drawn exclusively from web, or news content, however. If material matching your search does not make it into the top-20 results (for the former) or top-10 results (for the later), then you would not get an alert – so less well-optimised content could slip under the radar.

The main competitor for Google Alerts in this market is Yahoo alerts (http://alerts.yahoo.com/) (registration required). For some searches, it may be beneficial to run both at the same time (especially given differences in indexing across these two platforms). There are several other search and social monitoring services which offer email alerts as a means of keeping up with events which may be worth using, including:

Alerts.com (mobile market) (https://www.alerts.com/)
Giga Alert (subscription) (http://www.gigaalert.com/)
Topikality (semantic alerts engine) (http://www.topikality.com/)

Mailing lists and email newsgroups

Listservs, centrally organised email lists, have been a key part of journalistic newsgathering since email became the communicative medium of choice. Past literature in online journalism has focused heavily on Listservs; however, they are not without ethical considerations, nor controversy. The *Journalist* discussion group (whose technology rests on email contributions), established for left-leaning American journalists in 2007, was closed down due to the leaking of critical remarks against conservative figureheads by contributor David Weigel, who subsequently resigned his post. Listservs are for some still a crucial component of research and newsgathering, but it is not always clear where to go to find them (certainly most of the publicly collected lists on the web have not been updated since the mid-2000s).

Listservs are particularly popular within specialist communities, such as investigative journalism, and the following two are highly regarded therein:

Global Investigative Journalism Network (http://www.globalinvesti-
    gativejournalism.org/)
JOURNET (https://ls2.cmich.edu/cgi-bin/)

Callahan (1999) provides an extensive (if somewhat dated) list of listservs:

http://reporter.asu.edu/listserv.htm

Really Simple Syndication (RSS)

Taking the logic of 'push' technologies a stage further than email alerts, Really Simple Syndication (RSS) is perhaps the technology most closely aligned to the journalistic appetite for immediacy on the web. Put simply, RSS is a distribution technology which allows publishers of online content to instantly alert audiences when they have published new content.

In newsrooms up and down the country, organisations subscribe to Press Agency newswires which channel in breaking news from around the globe, provided to journalists via desktop applications. It is possible using RSS to develop a personalised newswire, helping journalists stay up to date with online news in their beat. This involves finding sources to follow, then setting up systems to follow them, usually via a feed reader or other RSS-compliant utility.

Most internet browsers allow users to store RSS subscriptions locally, and will even allow other programs, including email clients, access to these feeds across the web (even if the latest versions of leading browsers no longer offer RSS alert icons in their default view). But for optimum accessibility (including, in some cases, via mobile devices) stand-alone platforms have their advantages:

Bloglines (http://www.bloglines.com/) (web version only)
My Yahoo (http://uk.my.yahoo.com/)
Net News Wire (Mac – download) (http://netnewswireapp.com/mac/)
Netvibes (http://www.netvibes.com/en)
Reeder (mobile app) (http://reederapp.com/)
Tiny Tiny RSS (http://tt-rss.org/redmine/projects/tt-rss/wiki) (for mobile)
Windows Live (http://explore.live.com/)
Zite (http://www.zite.com/)

With the withdrawal of Google Reader in early July 2013, many journalists have been unsure about the best alternative RSS reader platform for managing their news agenda. Google Reader was arguably the most comprehensive and integrated of all readers and was very easy and efficient to navigate. Given this, it is little wonder that shortly after the announcement, two of the more popular alternatives both rely on Google Reader, either dependent upon its syncing engine, or owing a debt to its usability, 'feel' and functions. Given these connections to the defunct service, many users have taken advantage of the opportunity to seamlessly transfer their subscriptions over from Google Reader to these alternatives, which are:

Feedly (http://www.feedly.com/) (available as a browser add-on or stand-alone app)
The Old Reader (http://theoldreader.com/) (web-based browser)

RSS feeds come in many forms across the web and can be found using a range of methods for these two service, as for others. Here are some simple methods for finding and following online content using RSS:

> Many websites contain RSS feeds, but these won't necessarily feature in your feed reader's index. Look for the orange RSS button in your browser's address bar (in newer releases of Internet Explorer, you may need to display the *Command Bar* to seek out RSS). Alternatively, copy the RSS feed from the address bar and paste into your feed reader. When results are returned, some readers will indicate the number of subscribers that feed has. You may not know who they are, but their number may suggest how reliable the source is (and, importantly, whether or not the feed is still active).

> For some platforms, it is necessary to set up bespoke feeds (e.g. YouTube used to require URL hacking, in order to set up tag-based or search result RSS feeds). Feed generators for such sites are commonly available across the web and easy to find – simply search for Google *rss feed generator*.

> It is possible to 'scrape' updates from web pages which do not provide RSS by using services like Page-2-Rss (http://page2rss.com/).

In choosing a feed reader, it is wise to opt for a service which allows you to export all of your feeds, to save you the trouble of repeating the exercise in future.

The future of RSS?

The demise of Bloglines in September 2010 and Google Reader in early July 2013, not to mention the decision to remove the RSS icon as a default view from version 4 of Firefox (Orchard, 2011) have all led some to question whether RSS is still relevant, now that many people use Facebook and Twitter to keep up to date on news.

But it is very important to draw a distinction here; it is not the death of the technology itself which is implied by these recent events, RSS will continue to form part of the infrastructure which brings us news on any online platform. It is rather the death of consumer RSS readers which is suggested, something which has been addressed several times in the past few years (Diaz, 2009; Tartakoff, 2010; Kamen, 2011).

Whether or not there remains a viable commercial market for such readers, journalists, as professionals who deal primarily in information (one might add new information) will continue to be dependent upon such resources, along with technologists, researchers, publicity and marketing professionals, and government agencies.

But just because RSS readers are an important means of keeping up with the news today does not mean that they will always be available, and even if they are, it is important to recognise the limitations inherent to this method of newsgathering. In the wider scheme of a journalistic beat (whether regional or subject-specific), there will inevitably be many online sources which do not carry RSS, because they provide alternatives services (such as email alerts), or just because they have not enabled the technology.

Moreover, there are will be many beats for which there are few active and engaged online representatives, making crowdsourcing problematic. An alternative to available RSS feeds and crowdsourcing is therefore essential; the ability to scrape updates from websites becomes crucial.

At the most basic level, this would involve creating RSS feeds for web pages which do not have them. There are many options which will help here, including:

Feed43 (http://feed43.com/)
FeedFire (http://www.feedfire.com/)
Feedity (full functionality requires subscription) (http://feedity.com/)
FeedYes (registration required) (http://www.feedyes.com/)
Page-2-RSS (http://page2rss.com/)
WebRSS (http://www.webrss.com/)

But it is important to recognise the limitations of such services; most notably, they only give updates on what has been added and what is new, not what has been deleted, changed, removed or hidden. For tracking the full gamut of changes to online sources, it is necessary to employ what Calishain refers to as 'information traps' (Calishain, 2007).

These are effectively automated page monitors which track changes over time. There are a number of freely available (and subscription) web-based tools which can help here, including:

Watch that page (http://watchthatpage.com/)
Trackengine (subscription) (http://www.trackengine.com)
Change Detect (http://www.changedetect.com/)
Trackle (subscription) (http://www.trackle.com/search/)

There are also a number of browser extensions which perform a similar function, including:

Update Scanner Addon for Firefox:
(https://addons.mozilla.org/en-US/firefox/addon/update-scanner/)
Update Scanner Addon for Chrome:
(http://updatescanner.mozdev.org/drupal/content/)
Outwit Hub Firefox Addon:
(https://addons.mozilla.org/en-us/firefox/addon/outwit-hub/)

In addition, for those who are fully engaged in this approach to news-gathering online, there are in addition a number of more powerful client-side screen scrapers (or 'web data extraction' software), most of which require subscription. These are generally more configurable and customisable than web-based offerings; they are better at avoiding false-positive changes and minor changes than web-based trackers, and some (like Outwit Hub) can perform a number of other analytical functions too, which can be highly valuable in online investigations (such as offering advanced filtering and notification, scheduling and even support authorship of macros and 'regex', for bespoke scraping tasks, not to mention full technical support). These include:

Website watcher (subscription) (http://aignes.com)
Page Update Watcher (free) (http://download.cnet.com/Page-Update-
    Watcher/3000–2370_4–10468473.html)
Outwit Hub (subscription) (http://www.outwit.com/products/hub/)
ScreenScraper (http://www.screen-scraper.com/products/all.php)
Mozenda (subscription) (http://www.mozenda.com/web-data-scraping)

For further customisation and control over data scraping, it may be necessary to develop your own scrapers. This will involve learning programming code, whether iMacros (Schrenk, 2007) or Ruby

(Spradlin, 2009), or even a high-level coding language. Today, in cities up and down the UK, a healthy culture of social media events is bringing together journalists (hacks) and programmers (hackers), whereby programming can be applied to journalistic problems, and so journalists might learn some of the skills required in the information age. For guidance see Hackers/Hackers (http://help.hackshackers.com/).

There are ethical issues concerning screen scraping, aside from those issues which affect all informational resource. Extensive scraping of a website can place a burden on that site's servers and bandwidth, so professional screen scrapers will often contact the publishers of a site before starting work. Journalistic work in this area overlaps significantly with computer programming, for which reason an appeal to the ethical standards of this profession would be appropriate, especially the Association for Computing Machinery guidelines.

Newsgathering: a general framework

Once basic **push** and **pull** methods in online newsgathering are in place, it is necessary to consider what sources to follow. This can be a fairly subjective exercise. The following schematic is offered for the purposes of setting up a local newswire.

A model for hyperlocal online newsgathering: Rationale

The underlying philosophy behind this model is to look to the information outlets and sources in a local community 'beat' first, then follow up by finding these sources across the web. This approach is not presented as an alternative to conventional off-line news-gathering methods, nor as a replacement for them; there are not enough people or information sources online (and there likely never will be) for this to be a realistic goal. This model is presented as a tool which may help journalists...

To adapt from offline to online newsgathering.
To systematise news-gathering online.
To eke out stories which might otherwise be missed completely.
To reinvigorate their relationship with readers.

In the process, this system will re-calibrate the relationship between journalist and reader; the 'beat' becomes a 'social network', which is open to new forms of measurement, audit, review and analysis.

Application

It is essential to choose a taxonomy model which reflects the administrative bounds of the beat – in the case of a local reporter, the structure of the local authority is a good fit.

Once a model is established, keywords must be selected, which will be used to find sources and set up RSS feeds. For a geographical beat, this will necessarily include a full run-down of all local place names, but it will also (at different points in the news calendar) feature other terms too, including local people, organisations, companies, events, etc. Many sources will not require keywords, merely automated RSS feeds.

This structure must be kept up to date, as it is subject to change over time; it needs to reflect the shifting nature of people's lives.

Some online sources have no RSS feeds, and scraping feeds for these sources can be problematic. Once relationships are established with sources, a social network begins to develop; such that journalists may find news more efficiently this way, than via official sources. For these reasons, this news-gathering model must comprise three parts:

RSS feeds which are aggregated and filtered (in Yahoo Pipes, Feedrinse or similar),

A diary of sources which require systematic re-visit manually (ideally kept in a spreadsheet) and;

Membership of various social networks (including Twitter, Facebook, LinkedIn, Delicious, etc.).

1.   *Meta-sources*

Competitor news sources: Any beat will require several news search feeds – covering references to the local beat at local (competitor), regional, national and international news levels, and possibly references to the beat in the trade press too. Set up beat (and other) RSS feeds in:

Google News
Yahoo News
Bing News
Newsnow
Daylife

There will be some duplication, but this can be filtered out – ultimately these different services have different indexes, so it is important not to miss out
...if a subscription is available, then set up feeds in:

Factiva/Nexis etc.
Social news sites: of less importance to local journalism, but still worth monitoring:

Reddit
Stumbleupon
Digg

2. Administrative sources

Many 'official' news sources are available online, from local authorities to local single-issue charity groups. These can be organised accordingly:

Governance sources (the authorities)
Council website RSS feeds
Council newspaper sheet (likely require monitoring)
Council committee minutes – via Openly Local (if available)
Online Forward Plan (likely require monitoring)
Hansard (covered by They Work For You searches for place names and politician names within network) European Parliament (no feeds on site, advanced search necessary)
Freedom of Information – What Do They Know feeds for all local public authorities (NHS trusts, schools, council, etc.)

Political sources

Parish council (websites/SM groups, parish councillors across SM).
Local politics (committee SM groups, officers, councillors, mayor, opposition).
National politics (MPs, websites/SM presence party websites/SM presence).
International (MEPs websites/SM presence).
Policy areas (authorities and alternative voices)
Community: council social services, animal welfare groups, asylum groups, carer groups, children groups, women's groups, minority groups, Surestart, etc.

Leisure: local arts groups (theatres, arts centres, galleries, etc.), community centres, conservation groups, sports groups, teams and societies.

Health and social care: PCT management, carers groups, doctors GPs and hospitals, mental health groups, health awareness groups, patients groups.

Education and learning: Schools (primary, secondary, etc.), colleges, universities, council information, educational groups, teachers, parents associations.

Transport: transport committees and lobbies (motorists, cyclists, etc.).

Environment & planning: Planning committees, nimby groups, environment groups, big business.

Occupation/industry: employment agencies, business groups, businesses, local trade union reps, etc.

Law and order: council advice, local courts, local police services, neighbourhood watch groups, local lawyers/solicitors, Citizens Advice Bureau, local arbitration.

3. Social sources

For all social sources, think about who (individuals, groups) in conjunction with either where (geography of beat) or what (topic of beat), whichever is more apt.

Social Networks
  Facebook
    Search for and keep up with people, pages, groups and events.
    For people concentrate on searching by Location/Education/Workplace
    Speculative search using advanced search
    Public updates and conversations available in IceRocket or advanced search Google. Account required.
  Twitter *(and other microblogs and real-time services):*
    Set up place-name feeds.
    Set up geolocation search feeds (watch for limitations).
    Follow key/popular figures in beat, including famous sons and daughters (footballers, rugby players, other local celebrities – see knowhere and Wiki pages for suggestions).
    For generic Twitter search feeds, it may be necessary to filter for content that has been re-tweeted or which contain links, especially for breaking news.

Find followers in beat using geo-twitter and Tweepz searches (which provide feeds for new people).

Delicious
Sign up for tag-based RSS feeds. Quite a lot of companies, but the odd surprise. Account required.

LinkedIn
Keep up with companies within a beat
Search for and friend individuals working within beat. Account required.

Forums: Sometimes anonymity can be a strength, not just in terms of finding whistle-blowers, but also in contentious/competitive fields – the main weakness with forums can be lack of RSS). Try geographical terms in:

Omgili
Google Groups
Yahoo groups
Boardtracker
Boardreader
Possibly some other bespoke site (like Mumsnet).
Blogs and websites:
Blogs
Search for posts featuring local place names via Google Blog search, Icerocket, or Social Mention.
Search for bloggers whose About includes mentions of a local place name.
Websites
Conventional search in Google, Bing, Yahoo, Ask, Delicious, etc. for local place names.
Mutlimedia
Video
Youtube
Blinkx
Google Videos
Truveo
Images
Flickr
Panoramia
Twitpic (included in Twitter feeds)
Reference

Wikipedia: Set up searches to monitor all pages of interest in
  beat (places, people, subject matter, etc.).
Google maps: need to do this manually now, RSS on Google
  maps is no longer available.
Follow other local themes in web 2.0, as they arise:
  Crash map (http://www.crashmap.co.uk/)
  Crime maps (http://www.police.uk/)
  I want great care (https://www.iwantgreatcare.org/)

Getting organised

Once suitable sources for these themes (and types) are established, it is
necessary to differentiate between those which can be effectively found
online and those which cannot. Those which cannot will have to be
pursued via telephone, email and other offline methods. Those which
can be found online, require differentiating between those which can
be tracked using RSS and those which cannot. Those which offer RSS
can be followed in a feed reader. This is part of the news-gathering process which would ideally be shared within a team, and communicated
via a shared diary (or calendar).

Meanwhile, it can be useful to aggregate all of your beat feeds into
one place, where they can be filtered for non-relevant content, and
parsed of duplicates. Yahoo Pipes is the most robust (but by no means
the only) means of doing this.

Functions in Yahoo Pipes

The key modules for a simple Yahoo Pipe are:

Fetch feed: paste your RSS feeds in this box – use the + sign to add
  more.
Filter: filters out terms associated with places, events and issues you
  do not want coming back. For example, there is an Uxbridge in
  Massachusets – often referenced as Mass in blogs and news-copy.
  Use this module to block all references to this term.
Sort: this filter allows you to sort your content by publication date –
  obviously for a newswire, we need all content to be distributed by
  publication date.

Union: use this module to channel several fetch feeds together into
one output.
Unique: this filters out non-unique content, so if you find a story
from a local newspaper which also crops up in an aggregator feed
search, or in a blog search, it should not publish all three.

Join these all together into a logical flow, and finally connect to the
Output box, and with a little more tweaking, you should have your pipe
up and running.

References

BBC News (2011) Court results put on Twitter by West Midlands Police, BBC,
April 19: http://www.bbc.co.uk/news/uk-england-birmingham-13127533

Calishain, Tara (2007) *Information Trapping: Real-Time Research on the Web*. New
Riders: New York.

Callahan, Christopher (1999) *A Journalists' Guide to the Internet: The Net as a
Reporting Tool*. Allyn and Bacon: New York.

Carey, James W (1999) 'In Defense of Public Journalism', in Glasser, Theodore L
(ed.) *The Idea of Public Journalism*. The Guildford Press: London.

Castells, Manuel (2000) 'Material for an Exploratory Theory of the Network
Society', *British Journal of Sociology*, 51(1) (January/March 2000), 5–24.

Davis, Aeron (2000) 'Public Relations, News Production and Changing Patterns
of Source Access in the British National Press', *Media, Culture and Society*, 22,
39–59.

Diaz, Sam (2009) RSS: A good idea at the time but there are better ways now,
ZDNet, August 25: http://www.zdnet.com/blog/btl/rss-a-good-idea-at-the-
time-but-there-are-better-ways-now/23276

Department for Communities and Local Government (2011) Code of
Recommended Practice on Local Authority Publicity (The Publicity
Code), DCLG, March 31: http://www.communities.gov.uk/publications
/localgovernment/publicitycode2011

Fishman, Mark (1980). *Manufacturing the News*. University of Texas Press: Austin.

Foreman, Gene (2010) The Ethical Journalist: Making responsible decisions in the
pursuit of news. Wiley-Blackwell: Chichester.

Gilligan, Andrew (2009) The propaganda newspapers, The Evening Standard, July
27: The propaganda newspapers.

Haas, Tanni (2003) 'Importing Journalistic Ideals and Practices? The Case of Public
Journalism in Denmark', *The International Journal of Press/Politics* 8. 90–97.

Haas, Tanni and Steiner, Linda (2006) 'Public Journalism: A Reply to Critics',
Journalism, 7(2), 238–254.

Halavais, Alexander (2009) *Search Engine Society (Digital Media and Society Series)*.
Polity Press: London.

Halliday, Josh (2010) Digg investigates claims of conservative 'censorship', The Guardian, August 06: http://www.guardian.co.uk/technology/2010/aug/06 /digg-investigates-claims-conservative-censorship

Hansen, Kathleen, Neuzil, Mark and Ward, Jean (1998) 'Newsroom Topic Teams: Journalists' assessments of effects on news routines and newspaper quality'. *Journalism and Mass Communication Quarterly*, 75(4) ABI/INFORM Research, 803–822.

Harrison, Jackie (2006) *News.* Routledge: London.

Jarboe, Greg (2007) Revealing The Sources Of Google News, Search Engine Land, May 31: http://searchengineland.com/revealing-the-sources-of-google-news-11353

Kamen, Croc (2011) RSS Is Dying Being Ignored, and You Should Be Very Worried, Camenblog, January 03: http://camendesign.com/blog/rss_is_dying

McManus, John (1994) *Market-Driven Journalism: Let the Citizen Beware?* Sage: California.

MacDonald, A.M. (1977) *Chambers Twentieth Century Dictionary.* New edition. W & R Chambers: London.

Machill, M., D. Lewandowski and S. Karzauninkat (2005) 'Journalistische Aktualität im Internet. Ein Experiment mit den "News-Suchfunktionen" von Suchmaschinen', in M. Machill and N. Schneider (eds), *Suchmaschinen: Neue Herausforderungen für die Medienpolitik.* Berlin: Vistas, pp. 105–164.

Machin, David and Niblock, Sarah (2006) *News Production: Theory and Practice.* Routledge: London.

Morrison, James (2010) Spin, smoke-filled rooms, and the decline of council reporting by local newspapers: the slow demise of town hall transparency. Presented at the 61st Political Studies Association Annual Conference:Transforming Politics: New Synergies: http://www.psa.ac.uk/journals/pdf/5/2010/612_322.pdf

Ofcom (2010) UK Adults' Media Literacy Report, May 17: http://stakeholders. ofcom.org.uk/market-data-research/media-literacy/medlitpub/medlitpubrss /adultmedialitreport/

Orchard, Leslie (2011) What happened to feed auto-discovery in Firefox 4?, Decafbad blog, January 15: http://decafbad.com/blog/2011/01/15/what-happened-to-feed-autodiscovery-in-firefox-4

Orlowski, Greg (2003) Google News: press releases are OK – Official, The Register, April 05: http://www.theregister.co.uk/2003/04/05/google_news_press_releases/

Schrenk, Michael (2007) *Webbots, Spiders and Screen Scrapers.* No Starch Press: New York.

Spradlin, Justin (2009) Ruby Screen Scraping with scRUBYt!, JustinSpradlin.com, April 27: http://www.justinspradlin.com/programming/ruby-screen-scraping-with-scrubyt/

Tartakoff, Joseph (2010) The Death Of The RSS Reader PaidContent, September 10: http://paidcontent.org/article/419-the-death-of-the-rss-reader/

Thurman, Neil. (2011) "Making 'The Daily Me': Technology, economics and habit in the mainstream assimilation of personalized news". *Journalism: Theory, Practice and Criticism*, 12(4), 395–415.

Tuchman, Gaye (1972) 'Objectivity as Strategic Ritual: An Examination of Newsmen's Notions of Objectivity', *American Journal of Sociology*, 77(4), 660–679.

Ulken, Eric (2005) Non-traditional sources cloud Google News results, OJR, May 19: http://www.ojr.org/ojr/stories/050519ulken/

Zelizer, Barbara (2004) *Taking Journalism Seriously: News and the Academy*. Sage: Thousand Oaks.

8 Verifying online sources

The art of the online hoax

Journalists have been subject to hoaxes since the profession came to be. Sometimes hoaxers intended to change the course of history. In April 1887, the *Times* fell prey to one of the most infamous hoaxes of the 19th century, publishing fake letters purporting to show Charles Stewart Parnell's support for the Phoenix Park murders. On the other hand, some sophisticated hoaxes have been motivated by nothing more than the product of a bar-room bet. In 1953, The *Atlanta Constitution* carried a splash on a close encounter with extraterrestrial life. Two men had shot, shaved and cut the tail off a rhesus monkey, presenting what remained to the news desk as (late) life from Mars.

Debate abounds about the nature of such hoaxes, which in turn informs how journalists might deal with them. Some insist that the process of corroboration for online documents is materially different to the pre-online processes used, while others argue that there are offline precedents to all online hoaxes. This debate mirrors a much wider debate about the extent to which the internet is merely another tool for communicative purposes, or a new way of communicating. Friend and Singer (2007) suggest that we should position ourselves somewhere in the middle-ground, which is a pragmatic position to take.

The advent of the internet, and the increasing reliance we all have upon electronic documents for unearthing information both factual and trivial, requires that the age-old checks and balances journalists have always used to verify the authenticity of their sources need updating. Here follows a series of suggestions which can help journalists tell fact from fiction, find out who is behind an electronic document and, ultimately, help verify that document's authenticity.

Journalists often have to make snap judgements about the information contained in websites they use, and given how easy it is to replicate another website by lifting HTML code, this is a deeply problematic area.

Example: An unwelcome anniversary…

In December 2004, *BBC World* ran a story on the aftermath of the Bhopal disaster 20 years on from the tragedy. A leak of chemicals from a factory managed by Union Carbide (an American petrochemical company) late in 1984 led to the immediate death of 3,800 people, rising several thousands more in subsequent weeks and months.

In the intervening years, Union Carbide had been acquired by Dow Chemicals, whom a BBC journalist sought for interview. Unfortunately the journalist was fooled by a fake website run by anarchists The Yes Men, called dowethics.com. The journalist emailed the address on this site, and arranged an interview with the 'CEO of Dow Chemicals'. A Yes Men representative went on air live (masquerading as Dow's CEO) to publicly acknowledge Dow's 'responsibility' for the disaster causing an immediate loss of $2 billion from the share price of the company, and significant loss of face for the BBC (Wells and Ramesh, 2004).

Websites are a key source of information for journalists, but it is important to approach unknown websites with a healthy dose of scepticism. A helpful way for journalists to weigh up the veracity of a website, and one that should not prove onerous, is to employ the Journalist's Checklist…

Who…is responsible for the site? Is there an 'About' page, or an FAQ page which explains this? There may not be and of course in some situations it is perfectly reasonable and fitting that websites be published anonymously (especially when they are involved in whistleblowing). Nevertheless, if this is the case, this will necessarily impact its reliability as a primary source. If there is not one, ask yourself why not. If there is one, are the details included legitimate (try searching for an address, names, telephone numbers or anything else you can find using the various tools and methods elsewhere in this book).

Most reputable websites will have an About page, but if you are in any way suspicious, you can check ownership of a domain by searching in one of the many domain registration directories, such as domaintools' Whois Lookup (http://whois.domaintools.com/). Using the Whois domain directory, it is possible to find out the name (or names) in which a website was registered, the emails used to register it, the date when it was last registered, where it was registered and if you are prepared to pay a premium fee, you can even find out what other domains have been registered using the names you have found as registrant of the domain you are concerned with. This does not guarantee that the user has registered using legitimate information, and indeed it is possible and entirely legitimate to have some personal details hidden from public view from any Whois lookup service. But of course if this is the case, you may be drawn to certain conclusions about the reliability of the site in question.

What... is the nature of the site? If it is a corporate site, its purpose is to sell you something, whereas if it is a governmental site, its purpose is to inform (some might say persuade). Is it obvious from content on the site what its purpose is?

Understanding basic conventions in web addresses can help here, especially with regard to upper level domains. All British universities have web addresses which end in *.ac.uk*, and government websites end in *.gov.uk*. Knowing that companies trade in *.com* and *.co.uk*, while advocacy groups, NGOs and hobbyists often use *.org* domains can at least inform what you might expect from a website, at a very basic level. Stephen C. Miller developed a simple schematic (Miller, 2004) for determining the reliability for websites whereby government, then university domains are ranked most trustworthy (albeit with relativist caveats; such as excluding non-democratic governments, and accounting for personal use of academic domain space). Wikipedia offers an exhaustive list of domains:

http://en.wikipedia.org/wiki/List_of_Internet_top-level_domains

Why would anyone trust this site – how popular is it? It is relatively easy to establish how large online (US) audiences are for some websites. This can in turn suggest how reliable information shared on said site may be. Of course popularity is certainly not a fail-safe proxy for reliability and trustworthiness; after all most major news outlets widely regarded as among the most reliable sources on the web, have been duped and hoaxed at some point. We should be wary of equating credibility with online popularity as the only means of verification, for this form of 'pack mentality' is not fool-proof (Friend and Singer, 2007, p. 69). Nevertheless, if you have an idea of how popular a site is, this can add an extra dimension to the other means used to verify a claim made on a website.

Use the following tools to establish how big a site's US following are (albeit be aware that these statistics are based on extrapolation of those who 'opt in' to using tracking software and services online, so they contain a bias):

Alexa (http://www.alexa.com/)
Quantcast (http://www.quantcast.com/)

When searching for the official websites of corporations and other large organisations, it is always worth looking for them within public directories (like those introduced in Chapter 3 of this book). The veracity and reliability of information about websites in these directories is managed by real human beings, who are 'experts' in the fields they manage within the directory. Search engines cannot offer such protection, so there is at least a modicum or reliability about the results you will find here:

DMOZ Open Directory: (http://dmoz.org/)
Yahoo Directory: (http://dir.yahoo.com/)

If you are in any way suspicious of a site, especially in relation to what might seem like doctored or purloined graphics or images, check the source code of the site in question (right click on a page in any browser, and seek out 'view source' – you may then have to Control-F through the file, looking for file extensions, or duplicate code). If a site proclaiming to be a legitimate organisation has 'borrowed' from another site, or indeed if documents (say images for example) link through to other sites with an agenda, this might lead you to be sceptical about the authors.

Where can you find out what the website used to look like? The Way Back When machine (or Internet Archive) (http://www.archive.org/index.php) is a useful tool for prying into previous versions of web pages. This can be useful when pages disappear, move to new locations or change content. While it is possible to design web pages in such a way that their pages are not indexed by the Way Back When machine, and while it is possible for web authors to request that content be removed from this site, it can nevertheless be helpful for uncovering lost or unavailable material.

A similar (albeit far more restricted) means of accessing past pages of websites is in the cached option you often see associated with Google results. Click on these links to see what the website looked like when it was last indexed (website indexing can be up weeks out of date), which goes some way to explaining why from time to time you click on a page from your search results which do not actually feature the terms you've searched for – that page is gone!

When...was the site last updated? Some sites will contain dates on pages, others will contain upload dates within the HTML of their pages and others still contain dates in their web address (especially blogs). Google often includes a date of publication within search results for the web addresses of particular pages. In any case, reliability of online information is sometimes contingent upon timeliness, and there are other ways to check this.

By pasting the following javascript code into a browser, when looking at a particular page:

```
"javascript:alert(document.lastModified)"
```

..., it is sometimes possible tell when a site was last updated (albeit this will not work on some browsers, nor where a web page contains dynamic content, which discounts a lot of modern web pages). If you wish to monitor a page over time to see if it changes, you can subscribe to a service such as Change Detection (http://www.changedetection.com/) (or any of the screen-scraping tools featured in the previous chapter).

Sometimes you can tell a lot about a site by which other sites are linking to it, which is where *Open Site Explorer* (http://www.opensite-explorer.org/) can be a useful tool. Designed for webmasters who wish to check the link structure (and marketing) of their websites, this tool doubles up as a handy guide to who is linking to whom. Of course it is dangerous to presume online links are equivalent to an endorsement (many people link to sites they disagree with quite fundamentally). Nevertheless, all search engines use links to determine the PageRank of individual sites, and it is not uncommon for like-minded people to organise linking policies to improve their collective visibility in search (linking can be thought of as a form of social network). For this reason, Open Site Explorer (and to a lesser extent the *link:* function in Google search) are valuable tools in helping provide insight into those influences and lobbies which exist online, though neither can be considered to be comprehensive. As an alternative to Open Site Explorer, use Backlink Watch (http://www.backlinkwatch.com/).

Lastly, when a story appears too good to be true, try browsing for it through some of the established hoax-busting websites, to see if anyone else is discussing or alerting surfers to its unreliability:

Snopes (http://www.snopes.com/)
Urban Legends (http://urbanlegends.about.com/)
Museum of Hoaxes (http://www.museumofhoaxes.com/)

There are many ways to check the veracity of an internet source, but there is no substitute for the traditional and entirely healthy scepticism most journalists will take to finding any source they might consider using.

How to corroborate news websites

Example: The vanishing newspaper

In early 2010, a new weekly newspaper launching in London: *The London Weekly*. At the time (and, some may say ever since), it was not easy to find work as a journalist, and many job-seeking journalists wondered why so few friends and contacts in the industry had heard of jobs being advertised for this new paper. Some forensic analysis later (undertaken by James Ball, journalists at Journalism.co.uk, and Media Guardian, not to mention contributors on Media Guardian), it was discovered that the newspaper was an elaborate PR exercise, rather than the fourth estate it purported to be (Ball, 2010).

News websites (such as those covered in Chapter 7 of this book) are much like any other type of website when it comes to verification, and all of the approaches mentioned in relation to checking the veracity of websites more generally applies to this niche. However, there are one or two other factors suggested in the literature, which may merit further consideration. Cooke (2004) incorporates them into an extensive checklist for evaluating sources of news, reproduced in full here:

What is the purpose of the site?

What is the coverage of the site?

What topics are covered, and are they covered comprehensively?

Is the site an electronic version of a printed publication, or is it the site for a television or radio station? Does the site provide access to the whole content and if not how has the information been selected?

What is the reputation and expertise of any individuals or organizations involved in the production of the site? Is this an authoritative source of information?

What is the likely accuracy of the information?

Has the information been through any quality-control processes, such as refereeing?

Is the information likely to be biased by any individuals involved in its production?

Is there an explicit date for the information?

Is the information up-to-date?

When was the information last updated?

When will the information next be updated?

How frequently is the information updated?

Is there a statement of policy regarding the frequency of updating and the updating process?

Does the source need to be monitored or reassessed at a later date to ensure continued currency and maintenance?

Is the site easily accessible?

Is the information well presented and arranged?

Is the site easy to use and are there any user support facilities?

How does the site compare with other similar sites?

What is your overall impression of the quality of the site?

(Cooke, 2004, pp. 135–136)

How to corroborate social media accounts and blogs

Example: Going off message ...

In 2009, two students invented a fake Twitter account claiming to be then foreign secretary David Miliband. To make this profile as plausible as possible, they added comments patiently and accurately, monitoring the foreign secretaries real-world movements, and mirroring them in their tweets. That was until the death of Michael Jackson, when they made some altogether more newsworthy comments, catching out much of the UK press in doing so (Anderson, 2009).

Example: The joy of texts ...

Toothing is a digital means of engineering anonymous sexual encounters which relies on the short-range (often anonymous) messaging function available in Bluetooth technologies (such as Blackberries and Palmtop computers). However, it was first invented by TheTriforce.Com's Simon Byron, Ste Curran, and Dave Taurus, as a ruse to fool the media. The concept was brought to the masses in March 2004 with the creation of a Toothing Blog, a social network where the experienced and uninitiated could come together. Involving a cast of imaginatively named characters (including Toothy Toothing, from Tooting),

---

this 'community' was soon aided and abetted by curious and intrigued surfers from around the world, which in turn led to the establishment of further forums to serve the needs of Toothers internationally. Little wonder then, that the media would soon be drawn into this honey trap. In the month following the Toothing blog's debut, Reuters ran a lengthy article on the phenomenon, interviewing one of the hoaxers in the process. Wired News, *The Independent* (Arthur, 2004) and the BBC (Kelly, 2004) were also duped, and many of those who fell for it still had not acknowledged the fact a year later (Hanas, 2005), albeit perhaps with good cause.

Just as art imitates life, so the inverse is true of Toothing, which has subsequently moved beyond an acknowledged (and sometimes unacknowledged) urban myth into the realm of reality.

In some social media platforms, people can verify their social network accounts, but what if the news story in question is not contingent upon a celebrity or well-known figure? All social network accounts give off information trails (Bradshaw, 2009), and it is essential to approach these critically when trying to verify them. Here follow some suggestions for doing this.

All tweets have timestamps, which can be used to trace the origins of a story, and help establish whether someone was part of this story as it broke, or if they are coming to the story 'downstream'. Contextualising every tweet you find against a user's history is also important in getting a sense of who they are, what are their interests, what language they use, whom they interact with. Sometimes people set up hoax accounts by starting to comment on unrelated topics – make sure you check fully how far back a user's comments go, and how prolific they are.

Profile information in any platform is crucial to reliability – occupation and other biographical information are always important when reading texts for parody, sarcasm, irony, etc. However it is worth bearing in mind the nature of the medium. It is quick and easy to set up a Twitter account, and it is also much easier to have a one-to-many conversation with the world on this platform, than it is by using alternative social media, like Facebook. Twitter accounts with little history should therefore be taken with a pinch of salt. It is easy to tell how long a Twitter account has been going, for as with most aspects of the service, someone has invented a third-party service which does this for you (such as How Long on Twitter: http://howlongontwitter.com/).

It is important to check profile information against what a user tweets, and against what else can be found online about a given individual. It can be difficult to remember different usernames and passwords for different social media sites, and for this reason many people use the same names, nicknames and 'handles' across different sites, which can in turn be searched.

In Twitter, it is always helpful to source what other people are tweeting to the subject whose authenticity you are trying to check – use the advanced search command *to:(@username)* to find out (indeed many of the other advanced operators mentioned in Chapter 5 can be used to verify various aspects of a Twitter profile). This approach may give you an insight into friends in the real world too (though not necessarily), and may throw up evidence of veracity. But ultimately, directly interacting with the person behind the profile offers the most comprehensive means of proving their reliability.

Think about the age and demographics of the profile owner (much of which is covered in Chapter 5 of this book). Does the user communicate in teen-speak, or are they middle-aged and middle-class, precious with punctuation and formal in their grammar? Sometimes a professional will give away their trade in the technical language they use. Think about use of conventions. Twitter users know about hashtags, re-tweets, lists and other elements of the medium (such as Modified Tweets: MT), which we all have to learn. How likely is it that a novice Tweeter may use these elements?

It is always a good idea, when fishing for news in Twitter, to use an aggregator which instantly shows you the numbers of followers and followees a Twitter user has. The Twitter Search option provided by IceRocket (http://www.icerocket.com/) lets you browse over these numbers (hover your mouse over the number to the left of usernames). Such tools are ideal for weeding out spam, but they are also useful as a means of catching out online hoaxers.

Going further, to look at the names behind the numbers (of followers and followees), it is possible to see other hints about the trustworthiness of any given profile. If there are many obvious spam profiles among the user's follower, you can assume this user does not exercise quality control, and likewise, if they are following some random or unexpected accounts, you may draw your own conclusions.

There is no public, searchable directory of who owns blogs, nor blogging profiles; this would run entirely counter to the nature of the platform. However, it is sometimes possible to find out who a blogger is if they visit (and comment) on your own blog, if they have a blog of their own and use Google Analytics (the free web traffic metrics service) (Baio, 2011).

Wikipedia: curse of the obituarist

> **Example: Last of the summer wind-up**
>
> Following his death in October 2007, several national newspapers and media outlets ran with a surprising musical 'fact' from Ronnie Hazelhurst's impressively broad-ranging back-catalogue. Author of many instantly memorable sitcom theme tunes, including The Two Ronnies and Some Mothers Do 'Ave Em, he was, according to the obituaries columns of *BBC News*, *Guardian online* (Plunkett, 2007), *the Independent*, *The Times*, *The Stage and Reuters*, also author of S Club 7's 'Reach for the Stars'. Except that he was not – this gem was unearthed and regurgitated by many an obituary-writer, from a hoax entry in Wikipedia (Dick, 2008).
>
> In 2009, lightening struck twice, as various official obituaries for French composer Maurice Jarre, including those for *The Guardian*, *The Independent* and *The Sydney Morning Herald* carried quotes attributed to him, but which turned out to be the invention of a 22-year-old student at University College Dublin (Butterworth, 2009). Almost a year later, an unholy trinity was secured, when the authorship of '(There'll Be Bluebirds Over) The White Cliffs of Dover' was wrongly attributed to Norman Wisdom in several of his official obituaries, including those found in *The Guardian* and *The Mirror* (Orlowski, 2010), a 'fact' eventually sourced to Wikipedia.

In regard to all three of these hoaxes (and those inevitably yet to be published), it is worthwhile considering how Wikipedia determines its frame of reference. The following, from the verifiability page of Wikipedia Policy, is instructive:

> The threshold for inclusion in Wikipedia is verifiability, not truth – whether readers can check that material in Wikipedia has already been published by a reliable source, not whether editors think it is true.
>
> To show that it is not original research, all material added to articles must be attributable to a reliable, published source appropriate for the content in question. In practice you do not need to attribute everything. This policy requires that all quotations and anything challenged or likely to be challenged be attributed in the form of an inline citation that directly supports the material. (Wikipedia, 2011)

Ultimately, if a 'fact' is found on Wikipedia which is unsourced, it should not be taken at face value. The easiest method of verifying a reference found on Wikipedia is to seek out the *View history* tab (found on the top right-hand corner in every page of Wikipedia). Look down through the most recent changes, and check to see when the change you are concerned with was made, and who made it. If it is not possible to tell from the summary provided whether the excerpt has been changed or not, it may be necessary to manually go through the most recent changes – which can be time consuming for some of the larger (or more controversial) topics. As a quick shorthand guide, it is fair to say that the more recently changes took place, the more likely they are to be erroneous.

Each change in Wikipedia is associated with an IP address, and many with usernames. Wikiscanner (http://wikiscanner.virgil.gr/) offers one way of shedding light on who has been amending Wikipedia entries by the organisation they are associated with, though you have to search by subject or organisation (and associated IP range).

How to corroborate an email

Journalism is not just about getting out and 'finding' stories. Often stories find journalists, and email is one of the most convenient ways members of the public have of getting in touch. But how do you know when an email you have been sent is reliable or not? There are some useful guides available (BBC College of Journalism, 2011), and here follows some wider suggestions.

Language: Is the email written in a formal or informal way? What sort of words are used, and how are they used? How is punctuation used, and are there any obvious mistakes? In all cases answering these questions will give you an idea of how 'true' to the story your emailer is, and the extent to which they are who they claim to be.

Picture: Respond to your emailer asking them to send a picture of themselves – if they comply then they are more likely to be who they say they are. However, this means of verification can be problematic with breaking news.

People search: Where possible use a mix of proprietary and free online people-finders. In addition, think about your emailer's profile (and the context in which you are approaching them), and consider which social networks someone of that profile would most likely use, before undertaking a search. In short, it is a good idea to search for people by bearing in mind why they may be using the service. For a comprehensive list, see Wikipedia:

http://en.wikipedia.org/wiki/List_of_social_networking_websites

Detail: Always ask your emailer for more detail – any conflicting information may be helpful.

If you have undertaken all of these steps, and are still unsure, it can help to establish where an email has been sent from. Sometimes people will claim to be somewhere they are not, and such hoaxes can be easily spotted in a number of ways. For example, there are proprietary services which allow you to do this at a cost, such as eMailtrackerPro (http://www.emailtrackerpro.com/). But it is usually possible to check for this information free of charge. Use the following steps to verify an email sent to a Gmail account:

Log in to Gmail.

Open the mail whose sender's location you wish to query.

Click on the blue inverted pyramid on the right-hand side of the email navigation bar.

Click on 'show original'.

Look for line containing Received:from and look for IP address in square brackets (a series of four sets of numbers). If there is more than one, go through each, starting with the first; this is mapping out the route taken by each component within your email.

Ignore the domain name (which can easily be altered).

Search for IP addresses using a tracking service, such as IP-2-location (http://www.ip2location.com/).

It is important to note that this process is available in any email client which supports the viewing of email headers. Note also that emails sent from a Gmail user will not feature using this method within the Gmail client.

How to corroborate digital photographs

The sceptical among us knows that cameras lie, or at least, photo-editing software can help to pull the wool over our eyes. Media organisations have developed sophisticated checks and balances to help verify the flood of user-generated images (BBC College of Journalism, 2010). Nonetheless, so successful have some hoaxes been that we have a relatively new adjective for the process: to *photoshop*. And while some researchers have developed high-level software to help detect hoax multimedia (Zetter, 2007), it is nevertheless possible to use what is commonly available, when allied to sound editorial judgement, to do most of the fact-checking legwork you need.

Here follows some editorial and technical measures for use when it comes to verifying digital photography, to help journalists establish fact from fiction. If you receive an image via email, respond to the emailer asking to have a chat (via telephone). During the phone call ask the following:

What happened, what the image contains, and compare this with official sources for verification.
Who took the pictures, when and where. Check all of these details where possible (i.e. check names on the web, check when and where with official accounts etc.).
Where the accompanying email contains no text, or generic, non-specific text, then there's a good chance this is spam.

If the image contains any text or images, this should raise concerns. Beware of images contained in other files (Microsoft Word documents, PowerPoint, etc.) – as they may have been doctored. Considering the image, think about the qualities of the photography – does it seem too 'professional'? If it is a series of pictures, is it logistically feasible that the same person could have taken them all?

Beyond these editorial checks, it is helpful to check the technical specifications of the images you are concerned with. You will need access either to Photoshop, or to alternative photo-editing software. Check the dimensions of the image – anything less than 2000 x 1200 psi will more than likely not be the original digital camera image, but a compressed version – and if so, you might want to ask yourself why it has been compressed and sent in this form. Of course there are all sorts of valid reasons why it may have been doctored, but nevertheless this might give an insight.

Use your picture editor of choice to scrutinise the image. Using the zoom facility, inspect those areas of the picture where tones meet – you may see layers, or (suspiciously) straight lines, or pixelation (evidence of compression, which would imply a picture is not in its original state).

Perhaps the quickest, and most through way of checking for photographic hoaxes is to use a reverse image search engine such as Tineye (http://www.tineye.com/) or Google Search By Image (http://www.google.com/insidesearch/searchbyimage.html). Tineye lets you upload an image, which is then used to scour its extensive database of images – if the image you use is found elsewhere, Tineye will show you the site – then you can check its veracity, its timeliness and other elements.

If the image concerns breaking news, use popular real-time image search engines such as Picfog (http://picfog.com/), Twitpic (http://

twitpic.com/) and Yfrog (http://yfrog.com/) to see what else is being shared online.

The 'Properties' menu, accessed when right clicking on any saved image, can give away useful information about when and where an image was taken. Creation and modification dates, GPS co-ordinates and various other metadata are often available here, where digital cameras have been used. But it is also possible to find even more information about how, where and when an image was taken (not to mention the specification of the camera used), using bespoke software such as Exif Reader (for PCs) or EXIF Viewer (for Mac):

Exif Reader (program for PC) (www.takenet.or.jp/~ryuuji/minisoft/exifread/english)
GBO Imagehost (http://gbimg.org/)
Simple EXIF Viewer (program for Mac OS X) (homepage.mac.com/aozer/EV/)

The FXiF Firefox add-on (https://addons.mozilla.org/en-US/firefox/addon/fxif/) can also be used to check image metadata wherever you find them online.

However, a note of caution is necessary: it should be noted that this approach often yields inconclusive results. Research in 2009 showed that only 3.3% of images uploaded to various real-time image sharing services contain GPS coordinates (Flinn et al., 2010). If there is no Exif data associated with a digital image, then it is safe to say that the file was either taken with an analogue camera, or that it is a digital copy of an original, or that the camera owner has disabled some metadata capture. This does not mean it is not genuine, but it does mean you cannot verify its reliability without at least the help of other methods.

How to corroborate video files

As with images, all digital video is produced with operational metadata attached. As with images, some aggregators and platforms strip video of its metadata on upload, so it may not be possible to find in embedded material. But moving images can require a different level of analysis. It may be possible to find out if metadata information is available by trying any of the following pieces of (free) software:

Gspot (http://gspot.headbands.com/)

MediaInfo (http://mediainfo.sourceforge.net/en)
Video Inspector (http://www.kcsoftwares.com/?vtb#help)

At the BBC's User Generated Content Hub, staff double-check audience-submitted videos against places as they appear in digital maps, checking for shading and other visual clues for inconsistencies (Murray, 2011).

How to corroborate electronic text documents

> **Example: All things to oil men...**
>
> Some of the biggest news stories start their life buried away in text documents – this is something most investigative journalists will attest to. And when these documents are in electronic form, the metadata hidden behind the words can give an insight into the origins and veracity of a document. In 2005, it was discovered that a document contributed by climate sceptic Lord (Nigel) Lawson's to a US Senate environment committee was not authored by him, but by an employee of London PR company Luthar Pendragon, who was formerly a spokesman for Exxon Mobile. This became clear after journalists checked the document's metadata (Vidal and Adam, 2005).

The 'Properties' option in either Microsoft Word or Adobe PDF Reader will betray some useful information (such as when a document was created, or modified, or where a username is associated with a file). But sometimes it is necessary to delve deeper.

There are a various pieces of software which can be used to find much more metadata; some are suitable for Mac, others for PC:

Docscrubber (program, PC) (http://www.javacoolsoftware.com/docscrubber.html)
Oracle Outside In Clean Content (program, PC) (http://www.oracle.com/technetwork/middleware/content-management/cleancontent-094288.html)

Something Clean Content divulges, which Windows Explorer will not, the file path a file was saved in. Given that large organisations have large administrations, and that most employees have their own unique identities, it is possible to marry username and file path, and find out who else (perhaps unnamed in the document) may have been involved in its drafting.

Once the software is downloaded, you can verify documents using Clean Content by following these steps:

Run the program.

Choose 'Select and process a single document'.
Locate document, and click 'Next'.
Click 'Generate a risk analysis of the document…', then click 'Report!'.
A browser window will open containing the program's findings.
It is possible to view changes and comments on drafts of word documents from the File menu, but only where they have not been password protected.

References

Anderson, Kevin (2009) Fake David Miliband Twitter account dupes press, *The Guardian*, June 26: http://www.guardian.co.uk/media/pda/2009/jun/26/twitter-michaeljackson-davidmiliband-hoax-journalism

Arthur, Charles (2004) Tuned in, turned on, *The Independent*, April 21: http://news.independent.co.uk/sci_tech/article56861.ece

Ball, James (2010) The curious case of The London Weekly, JamesRB.co.uk, February 02: http://www.jamesrb.co.uk/?p=259

Baio, Andy (2011) Andy Baio: Think You Can Hide, Anonymous Blogger? Two Words: Google Analytics, Wired, November 15: http://www.wired.com/epicenter/2011/11/goog-analytics-anony-bloggers/all/1

BBC College of Journalism (2010) Hoax UGC Image Checks, BBC: http://www.bbc.co.uk/blogs/collegeofjournalism/skills/production/user-generated-content/hoax-ugc-image-checks.shtml

BBC College of Journalism (2011) Authenticating UGC Emails: http://www.bbc.co.uk/blogs/collegeofjournalism/skills/production/user-generated-content/authenticating-ugc-emails.shtml

Bradshaw, Paul (2009) How to spot a hoax Twitter account, Online Journalism Blog, October 16: http://onlinejournalismblog.com/2009/10/16/how-to-spot-a-hoax-twitter-account-a-case-study/

Butterworth, Sibiohan (2009) Open door: The readers' editor on … web hoaxes and the pitfalls of quick journalism, *The Guardian*, May 04: http://www.guardian.co.uk/commentisfree/2009/may/04/journalism-obituaries-shane-fitzgerald

Cooke, Alison (2004) *A Guide to Finding Quality Information on the Internet: Selection and Evaluation Strategies* (2nd edn). Library Association Publishing: London.

Dick, Murray (2008) Is the future in bits? *BBC News Magazine*, December 03: http://news.bbc.co.uk/1/hi/technology/7761153.stm

Flinn, Michael, Teodorski, Christopher and Paullet, Karen (2010) 'Raising awareness: an examination of embedded GPS data in images posted to the social networking site Twitter', *Issues in Information Systems*, XI(1), 432–438: http://www.iacis.org/iis/2010_iis/Table%20of%20Contents%20No1_files/432–438_LV2010_1370.pdf

Friend, Cecelia and Singer, Jane (2007) *Online Journalism Ethics, Traditions and Transistions*. ME Sharpe: New York.

Hanas, Jim (2005) UPDATE: Toothing Corrections? April 04: http://www.hanasiana.com/archives/000349.html

Kelly, Chris (2004) Biting into the new sex text craze, *BBC News Online Bristol*, May 07: http://news.bbc.co.uk/1/hi/england/3673093.stm

Miller, Stephen (2004) The Miller Internet Data Integrity Scale, *New York Times*: http://courses.ttu.edu/rreddick/ar/tools/MIDIS_handout.pdf

Murray, Alex (2011) #bbcsms: BBC processes for verifying social media content, BBC College of Journalism Blog, May 18: http://www.bbc.co.uk/journalism/blog/2011/05/bbcsms-bbc-procedures-for-veri.shtml

Orlowski, Andrew (2010) The Curse of Wikipedia strikes Norman Wisdom, The Register, October 06: http://www.theregister.co.uk/2010/10/06/wikipedia_norman_wisdom/

Plunkett, John (2007) Ronnie Hazlehurst – his greatest hits (obituary), *The Guardian*, October 02: http://blogs.guardian.co.uk/organgrinder/2007/10/ronnie_hazlehurst_his_greatest_1.html

Wells, Matt and Ramesh, Randeep (2004) BBC reputation hit by Bhopal interview hoax, *The Guardian*, December 04: http://www.guardian.co.uk/uk_news/story/0,3604,1366397,00.html

Vidal, John and Adam, David (2005) Eco Soundings, *The Guardian*, October 19: http://www.guardian.co.uk/society/2005/oct/19/environment

Wikipedia (2011) Policy page outlinging significance of verifiability: http://en.wikipedia.org/wiki/Wikipedia:Verifiability

Zetter, Kim (2007) Researcher's Analysis of al Qaeda Images Reveals Surprises – UPDATED, Wired.com, August 02: http://www.wired.com/threatlevel/2007/08/researchers-ana/

Index

Printed in China